GRIEVING FOR CHANGE

*A Spirituality for Refounding
Gospel Communities*

D0887984

Geoffrey Chapman Pastoral Studies Series

Making RCIA work, handling the management of change and loss, parish evangelization, diocesan renewal, moral theology at the end of the twentieth century, the challenges raised by *Christifideles Laici*, reconciliation, these are all issues to be covered in the Geoffrey Chapman Pastoral Studies series.

For the clergy, pastoral workers and interested lay people, the series is based on experience, and provides a comprehensive introduction to the issues involved.

The authors are recognized authorities on their subject and bring their considerable experience and expertise to bear on the series.

GRIEVING FOR CHANGE

A Spirituality for Refounding
Gospel Communities

GERALD A. ARBUCKLE, SM

GEOFFREY
CHAPMAN

Geoffrey Chapman
An imprint of Cassell Publishers Limited
Villiers House, 41/47 Strand, London WC2N 5JE, England

First published 1991

British Library Cataloguing in Publication Data
Arbuckle, Gerald A.
   Grieving for change: a spirituality for
   refounding gospel communities.
   1. Christian church. Change
   I. Title
   260

ISBN 0–225–66638–3

Phototypeset by Input Typesetting Ltd, London SW19 8DR
Printed and bound in Great Britain by
Biddles Ltd, Guildford and King's Lynn

CONTENTS

Acknowledgments   vii

Introduction   1

Part One: Understanding the group grieving process

1 Grieving in Gospel communities   11

  Case studies and reflections   12
  Sources of grief   19
  Stages of grieving   20
  Summary   22
  Discussion questions   23
  References   23

2 Letting go for newness: celebrating loss   25

  Understanding ritual's importance   26
  Insights from traditional cultures   27
  Case study: New Zealand Maori   28
  The twofold function of rites of passage   31
  Grieving: a social drama   32
  Case studies   37
  Summary   40
  Discussion questions   41
  References   41

3 Denying loss in Western cultures   43

  The American way of death: a case study   44
  Reactions to the denial of loss   53
  Summary   55
  Discussion questions   56
  References   56

Part Two: The grieving process in the Scriptures

4 'Call the mourning women . . .': loss and newness in the Old Testament   61

  Reflections on death and mourning rituals   62
  Psalms and laments: newness out of chaos   64
  The psalms in the social drama of life   68

Newness in the Book of Job   76
Jeremiah: prophet of grief and newness   78
Summary   81
Discussion questions   82
References   84

5 Jesus calls: mourn that we may be recreated   86

Dying/grieving for the kingdom   87
'Letting go' means mourning   88
'He has sent me . . . to comfort all who mourn' (Is 61:1f.)   93
'A man of sorrows, familiar with suffering' (Is 53:3)   97
'Near the cross of Jesus stood his mother' (Jn 19:25)   102
Summary   105
Discussion questions   106
References   106

Part Three: Initiating the grieving process

6 Death and newness in earthing the Gospel   111

Defining inculturation   112
The incarnation: the foundation model of all inculturation   117
Metaphors for inculturation: the earth, the sower and the
   seed   118
In inculturation cultures experience loss   122
Reflections on case studies   126
Summary   138
Discussion questions   138
References   139

7 Calling to mourn: leadership and refounding   140

'Refounding' and 'creative' persons as ritual leaders   141
Case studies   142
Official leaders as ritual leaders   150
Moses: an exemplar of the administrative ritual leader   151
Case study: the rites of passage of a Gospel community   156
Summary   159
Discussion questions   160
References   160

Epilogue   162
References   164

ACKNOWLEDGMENTS

I am indebted to many people and groups from a wide variety of cultures and nations who, over a twenty-five-year period, have shared with me their stories of grieving. A number of these stories are retold in this book. However, in order to protect the privacy of those involved, I have where necessary disguised their authorship by changing names and circumstances.

I am particularly grateful to the Scripture scholar Walter Brueggemann, because his inspiring books (e.g. *Hopeful Imagination: Prophetic Voices in Exile*) first gave me the idea to research and write on group grieving; to Mrs Ruth McCurry, editor of Geoffrey Chapman, London, for encouraging me to write the book; to several confrères of mine who have helped me with their particular professional insights: Jim Murphy, SM, Kevin Waldie, SM, and John Owens, SM. These people, however, can in no way be responsible for the book's inadequacies.

Excerpts from the New Jerusalem Bible, copyright © 1985 by Doubleday, a division of Bantam, Doubleday, Dell Publishing Group, Inc. and Darton, Longman and Todd Ltd, are used by permission of the publishers.

Refounding and Pastoral Development Research Unit
1 Mary St
Hunter's Hill, Sydney, NSW
Australia, 2110   March 1990

For:
Mary, Joseph, Teresa, Iris, Jane and Michael —
they grieve for newness

INTRODUCTION

Suppressed grief suffocates (Ovid, *Tristia*, book V, eleg. 1, line 63).

As a little boy of nine I would deliver newspapers daily to subscribers in my small village in New Zealand. Each day I would meet an elderly Christian Maori chief, who would be standing silently before a tribal meeting house faced with wooden carvings depicting his ancestors and the former greatness of his culture of pre-colonial days. He would break from his contemplation to greet me warmly but gently.

I looked forward each day to that smile and being treated as though I were an elder myself. Only later did I realize the source of his warmth and why he would stand before the carvings each day. He was grieving over the loss of the identity and sense of belonging of his people. Yet as he pondered this loss, sometimes even in tears, a new life would take hold of him. He would identify the sufferings of his people with those of Christ and believe that through his Savior's resurrection he and his tribe would discover a new heart, a new strength. New leaders would emerge to evoke a revitalized sense of tribal self-worth through ways radically different from those of their ancestors. He did not know when this would happen. But the more he acknowledged the death of the old, the more he hoped. The elderly Maori chief, Waimarama Puhara, is long dead, but his message is as fresh in its relevance to us today as it was for his own people in the 1940s.

Gospel communities experience loss

Let me explain. We Christians today, especially in the Western world, can suffer much loss personally and also as apostolic groups or communities: the loss of our once-powerful influence within Western society; the decline of the control of the Western Churches over the congregations they established in the so-called mission and colonial countries; the closure of parishes and churches because there are too few parishioners to maintain them; the disappearance of prayer and liturgical structures that have existed for centuries; the loss, or threatened loss, of male dominance in ecclesiastical ministry and government as the call for women's rights gathers momentum; the withdrawal of religious congregations from the ownership or direction of hospitals and schools—because these same congregations are numerically in decline and may even face death within a few decades.

Some accept losses like these happily and creatively, others feel sad and disoriented by them and do not know how to relate to them constructively. Others deny that losses have occurred at all and refuse to grieve over them; yet, deep down, they are in pain. My friend Waimarama Puhara did not deny the painful cultural malaise into which he and his people had fallen. On the contrary, the more he acknowledged the pain the more he found meaning and hope in the sufferings and resurrection of Christ.

However, the greatest sadness we should all experience as evangelizers is not only our own sinfulness, but also the loss of interest by the world in the message of Christ. Secularism is alive and well and all the old ways of evangelizing seem powerless to stem secularism's attractiveness for people. Our churches are quaint reminders of a world that is gone; in the eyes of many, we are useful for providing charity for the poor, nothing else. We are irrelevant. We must grieve over the fact that we have contributed to the alienation of peoples from Christ through our own reluctance, as individuals and as evangelical communities, to co-operate with the Holy Spirit calling us to innovative pastoral action. Christians have often, though sometimes unconsciously, supported sexist, racist and other structures that are thoroughly contrary to Christ's teaching. Opportunities have been repeatedly lost to preach Christ's message of love and justice. There is much to grieve over.

We can, however, become so overwhelmed by these losses that our hearts become numbed and our energies drained by the struggle to restore that which has been irretrievably lost. And we can even deny that these losses have occurred at all.

Need for a spirituality of grieving

I believe we desperately need a spirituality that helps us to acknowledge the death of the once-powerful social status of the Churches in society, and the irrelevancy, even the injustice, of attitudes and structures that are obstacles to the contemporary proclamation of the Word of God. As long as we individually and as communities refuse to grieve over that which is lost or now apostolically irrelevant or unjust, we will not let go of the past. Thus we will be refusing to make room for much-needed apostolic resurrection, freshness, and innovation.

Let me explain this further. Much has been written in recent years on the necessity for individuals to learn the art of grieving about significant losses in their lives. But almost no literature exists about the fact that all kinds of apostolic groups or Gospel communities (for example, families, parishes, Basic Christian Communities, dioceses, hospitals, schools, religious houses, and provinces) do themselves experience bereavement or loss, and must learn to cope with it positively through a process of grieving. This book concentrates on *why* apostolic groups, organizations or cultures, and not only individuals, must learn to grieve over, and not deny, what has been lost or has become pastorally irrelevant. It also proposes an appropriate spirituality to assist Christian communities to let go of the past in order to allow the new to enter.

Why is there such a dearth of literature on this critical issue of why group grieving is necessary, if there is to be new life? Among the reasons given in subsequent chapters there is one that is particularly important here. The fact is that rarely do we consciously feel the presence and power of culture, so we fail to see the reason why groups or organizations should grieve over loss *before* there can be newness of apostolic vitality.

Let me briefly clarify what we mean by culture. Each apostolic group, like every human organization, has a culture unique to itself. That is, every group of people share to some degree or other similar ways of looking at life through particular symbols, myths, and rituals. A culture is very much a 'silent language',[1] because people are rarely conscious that a culture's traditions and conventions actually exist—or powerfully influence their attitudes and actions. In a very real sense, every culture has a life that is more than the total of all the individuals that adhere to it, because, though a culture lives *in* individuals, it also *transcends* them at the same time. A culture does not die when individuals die; it lives on to influence subsequent generations of people. And normally there is no simple and quick method whereby individuals are able to counter a culture's potential to affect their lives. As Alan Kantrow says, just as an oil supertanker under full power cannot stop on a dime or turn on a nickel, so also the silent juggernaut of culture is no different.[2]

Sometimes, in order to highlight this person-like quality of a culture, expressions like 'group-think' or 'corporate person' are used instead of the word 'culture'. Like the human being, a group or corporate person is born, develops, suffers, and may even evade or deny loss and die.[3] The Israelites of the Old Testament times recognize the corporate and developmental qualities of a culture. They see themselves not just as individuals, but as a nation or corporate person that rejoices in Yahweh's favor, that suffers and denies the loss of Yahweh's friendship through sin and exile. Sometimes as a nation they learn to acknowledge their failures and grieve over them, thus experiencing new energy through a life of justice and love toward Yahweh and the poor.[4]

Division of this book

The book is divided into three parts. In Part One basic terms like grief, mourning, and bereavement are defined, and practical illustrations are given of the types of losses, and the reactions to them, that contemporary Gospel communities may undergo. With the aid of various social sciences, especially cultural anthropology, we see how cultures can either deny or acknowledge death. In the modern Western world not only do our cultures help to blind us to the reality of death or of any significant loss, but they also deprive us of those structures that in traditional cultures can support the grieving process. We must turn to traditional cultures, for example the Israelite culture of the Scriptures, to relearn the art of grieving.

Both Old and New Testaments, as is explained in Part Two, are a rich resource for discovering what a spirituality of corporate grieving or of letting go should mean today. Practical guidelines are provided in Part Three about ways to foster this spirituality within Gospel communities, that is, within all kinds of communities that aim to live out the life, death, and resurrection of the Lord, such as families, parishes, mission organizations, religious congregations, staffs of schools, or hospitals.

The subtitle of the book speaks of a spirituality of *'refounding* Gospel communities'. The use of the word *refounding* may at first surprise readers, but the word best summarizes the challenge now confronting us as Christians. A brief reflection on the last three decades supports this assertion.

Back in the 1960s there was tremendous optimism and euphoria among Christians, especially among those belonging to the mainline Churches, as a result of the refreshing openness of the Vatican Council for Roman Catholics and the revitalized dynamism of the World Council of Churches. Centuries-old barriers that had separated Christians came tumbling down, the Churches challenged the faithful to let go of their inward-looking or ghetto mentality and to commit themselves to struggle for peace and just political and economic structures in the world; 'renewal', 'unity', 'dialogue', and 'social justice especially for the poorest' became the dominant expressions of the decade. Everything seemed right for a massive rejuvenation of Christian communities throughout the world.

The renewal of Christian communities as powerful agents of evangelization has succeeded only to a very limited degree. Over all, Gospel communities are confused, even in chaos, about how to evangelize a world that is in tumultuous change at all levels. As we lurch towards the year 2000 we are beset by ever more alarming reports of ecological disasters, from deforestation in Brazil to the Philippines and massive regular floods in Bangladesh, to the 'greenhouse effect' and acid rain. Add AIDS and the chronic poverty and oppression in the Third World, the irrelevance with which people view the teachings of Jesus Christ and the Churches, and it is not hard to see why apocalyptic visions are currently fashionable.

Reactions to these apostolic challenges differ among Christians. Some of us nostalgically gather together to revive apostolic methods and liturgical practices of old, which are totally out of touch with Christ's call to evangelize the world as it is today. Others retreat into a private or sect-like fundamentalist religion which refuses any involvement with the mission of Christ to the world.

We desperately need new organizations, structures, and methods of evangelizing a constantly changing world. So enormous is the challenge that no longer is the phrase 'renewal of the Church or faith communities' adequate to convey the immensity of the task facing us. The process of refounding, that is, of finding and implementing new methods of bringing the faith/justice Good News to the world, is more akin to the phoenix—a rebirth—than the gentle, refreshing breeze that 'renewal' has come to connote.

There are people—all too few as yet—who, filled with Christian hope, are involved in refounding Gospel communities in this way throughout the world. They are to be found in divers apostolic ventures: there are those who risk their lives in the struggle for Gospel justice in frontline political action or in the slums of countries as diverse as the Philippines and the United States; they are teachers who daily strive to find new ways to preach Christ's message of saving love in the classroom or university lecture hall. They are parents who set an example of love and justice within cultures hostile or apathetic to Christian family life; they are managers and employees in multinational industries who demand that their employers act according to the principles of social justice and not unbridled capitalistic competition. They are the hidden individuals and groups who give their lives over to prayer that people may become open to the mercy and compassion of an ever-loving Lord; they are women in cities and remote villages, who persistently and non-violently press for political, social, and economic equality within societies dominated by superior-conscious men.

The action of refounding is a co-operative effort in which prophetically imaginative and creative persons unite with administrators and others to build new, or to revitalize existing, communities, under the inspiration and sustaining power of the Holy Spirit, through which Christ is brought anew to the world.

One essential task of these communities is constantly to grieve in faith, prayer, and action over their own sinfulness, their loss of opportunities to preach the healing presence of Christ, their hesitancy to let go of evangelical attitudes and structures that simply are now inappropriate, or even harmful, to the apostolate. They are then always open to the creatively new in the service of the Lord and the world. The act of calling communities to grieve is a crucial one for leadership and a chapter is devoted precisely to this.

This book is a sequel to three other books that I have written on the challenges and problems of change confronting various types of Gospel communities, especially within religious congregations.[5] At times in this book, in order to give a realistic context to what I say on the spirituality of grieving and refounding, I summarize key conclusions of these other studies. However, readers may find it helpful to return to these books in which the conclusions are explained more fully. Relevant references are provided in the end-of-chapter notes.

References

1. See E. Hall, *The Silent Language* (New York: Doubleday, 1959), *passim*.
2. *The Constraints of Corporate Tradition: Doing the Correct Thing, Not Just What the Past Dictates* (New York: Harper & Row, 1988), p. 63.
3. For an explanation of the cultures of organizations, their power over the individual and their life cycle, see M. Douglas, *How Institutions Think* (Syracuse, NY: Syracuse University Press, 1986), *passim*; D. Graves, *Corporate Culture: Diagnosis and Change* (New York: St Martin's Press, 1986), pp. 25–51; E. H. Schein, *Organizational Culture and Leadership: A Dynamic View* (San Francisco: Jossey-Bass, 1987), *passim*; D. Schon, *Beyond the Stable State* (London: Temple Smith, 1971), *passim*.
4. See W. Brueggemann, *Hope within History* (Atlanta: John Knox Press, 1987), p. 74 and *passim*; H. W. Wolff, *Anthropology of the Old Testament* (Philadelphia: Fortress Press, 1974), pp. 214–22.
5. *Strategies for Growth in Religious Life* (New York: Alba House, 1986; Middlegreen: St Paul Publications, 1987); *Out of Chaos: Refounding Religious Congregations* (New York: Paulist Press; London: Geoffrey Chapman, 1988); *Earthing the Gospel: An Inculturation Handbook for Pastoral Workers* (London: Geoffrey Chapman; Maryknoll, NY: Orbis Books; Sydney: St Paul Publications, 1990).

PART ONE

Understanding the group grieving process

Give sorrow words: the grief that does not speak
Whispers the o'er-fraught heart, and bids it break
(Shakespeare, *Macbeth*, IV, iii, 209).

Chapter 1

GRIEVING IN GOSPEL COMMUNITIES

Grief makes one hour ten (Shakespeare, *King Richard II*, I, 3, 261).

In this chapter I shall explain briefly the nature of grief, and its various forms, causes and stages. This explanation will be illustrated through the use of case studies that recount how some individuals and contemporary Gospel communities react to grief.

Grief describes the sadness, sorrow, confusion, even guilt, that can emerge when individuals or cultures of all kinds suffer a loss. The frequent experience of loss—for example, the loss of one's youth or the power to decide things for oneself—is an inevitable and normal part of the human condition, one of the innumerable 'slings and arrows of outrageous fortune'.

Sometimes it is thought that grief occurs only when one loses a loved one. This is incorrect, though the way we relate to the loss of a loved one is the model according to which all other types of loss are structured. Several years ago I spent three months recuperating after a sudden serious illness. This demanded that I cease an intensely busy schedule of administration and lecturing. During the early stages of the recuperation period especially, I felt bewildered, ill-at-ease or restless, even fearful, without knowing quite why this was so. Then I stumbled on the words of C. S. Lewis which describe his grief after the death of his wife: 'No one ever told me that grief felt so like fear. I am not afraid, but the sensation is like being afraid. The same fluttering in the stomach, the same restlessness, the yawning . . .'[1] These words articulated perfectly my own feelings, because though I had not lost a loved one I had definitely lost my good health, and with it my valued and satisfying work. I was in grief and I had not realized it.

The word *bereavement* is generally used to describe the state of being lost or in grief; the term *mourning* is usually reserved for the social, visible, or conventional expressions of grief. The ways in which people are expected to mourn (or not mourn) are strongly influenced by their culture.[2]

Throughout this book I use expressions like *grieving over* or *rituals of grief*; normally these phrases signify the fact that positive attempts are being made to cope with grief. John Bowlby considers that the process of grieving and mourning is positive if there is a successful effort by an individual 'to accept both that a change has occurred in the external world and that he is [thus] required to make corresponding changes in his internal, representational world and to reorganize, and perhaps to reorient, his attachment behavior accordingly'.[3] The same can be said of any culture or organization that experiences grief.

The following are biographies of individuals/cultures illustrating ways in which they react to incidents of loss. I would suggest that the stories be read slowly to allow readers time to identify, as far as it is possible, with the diverse emotional reactions of the people affected by the losses. I comment on these reactions at the end of the case studies.

CASE STUDIES AND REFLECTIONS

1. The grieving parishioner

'I am now in my fifties. When all the liturgical changes came in after Vatican II, I was very happy. How good it was to hear the prayers in English and to learn about how we share in the priesthood of Christ, how we must bring the Gospel of justice to a world in change! In those days I never thought about what we were giving up. In fact, the changes were sudden and we felt the old ways of doing things were wrong. Now I find myself—with so many of my friends—at times yearning for the old days when everything was clear about what we had to believe and do in the Church. I look back to the time of Father X, a saintly man, and to the Sunday evening devotions. Sometimes we all feel angry, even depressed, about all the changes. Certainly I want the parish to settle down. And so do others.'

2. The displaced parishioner

Mr X had belonged for many years to an inner-city parish closed down by Episcopalian authorities because the majority of the parishioners had moved to outer suburbs. Mr X comments on his reactions to the closure: 'One Sunday two years ago during the regular service, we were told from the pulpit that it had been decided to close the parish. This was the first we had heard of it. We were all stunned. They said it was for the sake of "pastoral efficiency"! Within a month the church doors were closed for good. There was no service to mark the occasion. We were just told to worship in the next parish.

'I did go—at first—but I felt so ill-at-ease, even angry, because I could recognize no familiar faces. People would leave the service, jump into their cars and leave me cold and lonely. And there are no devotional shrines at the new parish church. I feel without them I have lost something of myself, for I loved those devotions. Others feel the same.'

3. 'No-nonsense grief'

A clerical religious province decided at its congregational provincial chapter to move out of a college that had been its 'pride and joy' for many decades. The provincial notified the bishop that the congregation would turn the school's management over to the laity and all religious would withdraw within twelve months. The provincial instructed religious teachers to show the laity what 'true sacrifice and dedication is all about. We religious must show others what our spirit of simplicity means.'

The religious were 'to work hard up to the last day and depart with a "minimum of fuss" '. This they duly did. No time was set aside for formal and protracted farewells to the college community.

The religious, many of whom had worked for years at the college, were immediately assigned to other apostolates. Several of these religious have 'not settled down' in their new work. They feel angry and sad about how the withdrawal took place. One described his experience in this way: 'I went along with the "no-nonsense" approach. But even after several months in my new job, I keep waking up at nights feeling angry and tense without quite knowing why. If only we could have said goodbye to the school before we left it! If only the school could have farewelled us!' Another said: 'Some of us who transferred to new jobs keep blaming our new communities for our feeling of misery. When I think about it, it does not make sense. They have done nothing wrong. But why do we feel so angry with everybody?'

4. The grieving religious

Sister X, aged 60, a trained teacher, belongs to a province in which the average age of the sisters is 64. She comments: 'I have long rejoiced in the changes that Vatican II brought to religious life. Now, however, I feel confused. There are no vocations to our province. We are certainly dying out as a province and as a congregation. This upsets, even hurts, me deeply at times. As I look to the future I feel numbed. There is no one to take my place and, to be honest, no one to look after me. I am dreading old age. As a province we are drifting, believing unrealistically at chapters that something will turn up to solve our problems. The whole thing is getting me down. I am beginning to feel that we should go back to the old ways; then we might get vocations. I really feel there is no future for me. To make matters worse, I have just retired from years of teaching. I loved teaching. It gave me a reason to exist.'

5. A religious province in denial

A major superior opened the chapter with a detailed report on the state of the province. With the skilled use of statistics he showed that the congregation must within the next four years withdraw from several parishes and schools, simply because the province did not have the religious to staff them. The chapter was asked to consider the report thoroughly and make the necessary decisions to withdraw. The chapter, however, refused to do so. Having approved the superior's report, the chapter proceeded to discuss matters of incidental importance. One observer later noted:

> The chapter was stunned and benumbed by the enormity of the loss to be experienced by the congregation over a short period. It sought escape by denying that the shortage of personnel even existed. At various points, chapter members blamed the superior for 'lack of leadership' and for 'the poor morale of the province'. They also at times criticized the research worker, who had prepared the material for the provincial's report, claiming he 'lacked expertise'. One delegate received very warm support for his view that 'we must trust far more in Providence for God will see us through the temporary [sic] shortage of personnel'. Decisions were made to return to some past ways of doing things. Then, it was said, 'the old ways will bring back the success of the past and if we pray harder any problem will disappear'.

6. The reluctant foreign missionaries

A Protestant missionary organization was established in England in the nineteenth century to foster the development of their Church in newly colonized lands. The success of its work is obvious: local congregations have ample recruits to the ministry, schools are flourishing. However, English ministers are still vigorously holding on to positions of administration at all major levels. One English administrator who has worked all his life in one of the congregations comments: 'We have been here for over a hundred years. Let's face it, we know how best to lead these people. They need us for a long time to come.' On the other hand, one indigenous minister expresses how he and other local ministers feel: 'The foreigners have done a good job—in the past. They don't know when to leave and hand over to us. We have the talents to direct our own affairs. Their models of worship and administration are Western. We want to develop our own, but as long as the foreigners think they are indispensable, we cannot do it. We are made to feel inferior.'

7. A culture in grief

Maori are the original Polynesian inhabitants of New Zealand. Maori feeling of cultural identity and self-worth has been radically undermined as a result of prolonged contact with the culture of European immigrants and their descendants for over 150 years. 'We became', said one Maori, 'strangers in our own land. Our culture was destroyed. We drifted into the cities in search of life and identity, but we found nothing, often only a feeling of despair. We were told by whites that our culture was worthless. We looked for understanding, but rarely found any. Often our white Christian pastors could not understand our suffering and yearning for the old ways. They kept saying: "Face reality and stop feeling bad. You would have been worse off if we white people had not come." They simply could not understand the sadness we feel.'

8. Rational planners

A religious congregation recognized that it could no longer staff several of its schools because of a dramatic decline in recruitment to the order. It was decided to withdraw over a period of ten years from the majority of the schools, some of which the congregation had founded many decades ago, and to hand them over to lay direction. This decision was communicated to the schools' staffs and the respective associations of former pupils.

The sad, and at times bitter, reactions of these associations to this decision startled members of the congregation. One congregational administrator who had been involved in the decision expressed her surprise: 'Their vigorous attack on us is impossible to explain because the decision to leave is so obviously rational and logical. Why can't they see this!' On the other hand, a former pupil commented: 'When the congregation pulls out something of ourselves and former generations is destroyed. We are angry because we have lost something and the congregation simply does not understand and want to listen to our hurting. We were never involved in the decision to withdraw the religious. How can they be so arrogantly insensitive!'

9. A nation denies loss

In 1915, during the First World War, Australian and New Zealand troops landed at an extremely inhospitable beach, called Gallipoli, in the Dardanelles, in an effort to push back the Turkish enemy, but they were defeated. It was a horrendous military mistake and thousands died simply because of the poor planning and supervision of the venture. However, the unredeemed squalor, horror, and futility of the Gallipoli campaign was officially ignored, and all the public ever came to know was the extraordinary bravery and fighting spirit of the troops. Those who survived were never encouraged to speak about the losses resulting from the demented recklessness of the battle's planners back in London. The Churches did nothing to bring the real truth out as they also became swept up in a false patriotism.

An 84-year-old veteran was recently interviewed and one senses the righteous anger coming from long officially denied grief: 'The fact is that we were led up the garden path. No one wanted to admit it then or later. I have waited 70 years for the truth to be told, which it's never been, and if I live to see the day perhaps I will die less angry.'[4]

All the people or cultures in these case studies are showing symptoms of experiencing significant loss. In some instances people have been physically separated from long-established groups (for example, the pre-Vatican II Church, a parish, a successful college, a thriving province, a culture that gave a sense of identity and self-worth), yet in their hearts they remain attached to these groups. They are lonely, hurting. No person of authority seems aware of this fact; nor has there been any formal public ritual acknowledging that loss has occurred. Maori people in case study 7 are in pain, because their traditions have been destroyed and they feel that few evangelizers in the white dominant culture understand their grief.

In case study 9, congregational administrators are unaware of the fact that grief is a deeply emotional experience; it is not something that can be prevented by cool, logical, and rational arguments. No effort was made to anticipate and articulate the grief of former pupils of the schools. The decision to withdraw had been made and that was all that was necessary, or so the administrators thought.

The case studies illustrate various forms of grieving being experienced at the individual and group levels. Notice that when individuals speak they are often articulating what others are also feeling. In case study 4, the sister experiences some typical symptoms of dramatic loss: confusion, numbness, sadness. She is discovering that her days of active apostolic life are numbered. She also has *anticipated* grief for she worries about the further losses the future will bring—for example, through her own aging and the decline of her own congregation. One senses also a developing *chronic* grief, because she anticipates that there is no way out of her grief and its accompanying depression. She begins to seek nostalgic refuge in the pre-Vatican II ways of being a religious. Miss Havisham, the deserted bride in Charles Dickens's *Great Expectations*, knew this form of grief. She sat for years in her fading wedding gown surrounded by the ruins of her wedding reception; all the clocks of the house had been stopped at 'twenty minutes to nine'. Chapter delegates in case study 5 also have anticipated grief; they look into the future and already begin to feel the enormous sadness that comes from having to withdraw from their parishes and schools.

The parishioner in case study 1 has *delayed* grief. No public ritual had taken place to help her to realize just what she was losing by moving into the Vatican II parish life. As the years went by, she felt as if she had lost something important through the many changes; she yearned for the time 'when everything was clear about what to believe and do in the Church'.

The teachers who moved out of the school in a 'no-nonsense way' (case study 3) have *delayed* grief. That is, they were kept so busy right up to the departure from the school, that they did not have time to think about what was happening. Only later in their new appointment were they confronted with the reality of their loss and how it had occurred. Some are suffering *inhibited* grief since they keep blaming in an irrational way the superior and community to which they now belong; they cannot see the real source of their hurting. Inhibited grief is also evident among chapter delegates in case study 5, since they quite unreasonably and wrongly blame their superior and the researcher for the problems that the province faces.[5]

Another form of grief is termed *bereavement overload*; individuals or cultures experience loss from many quarters at the same time. The amount of pressure on the bereaved can be far too devastating for them to handle all at once for a long time to come. The sister in case study 4 is simultaneously being bombarded by several personally significant losses: the loss of her job and the death of friends. Similarly, in case study 5 chapter delegates are quite overwhelmed on discovering the enormity of the effects of the decline in their province's workforce, so they seek effective refuge through a massive denial of reality.[6]

I have included the case study of the Gallipoli campaign tragedy from the First World War to illustrate that nations can for decades refuse to acknowledge an immense and tragic loss of thousands of young men. It also shows that the Australian and New Zealand Churches have shared in this denial. If ever veterans did try to speak of what really happened, they were so often disbelieved that they would fall silent. They desperately felt the need for a public ritual of mourning in which the sordid truth could be acknowledged; since this has not happened their anger has remained *suppressed* and the nations have missed the chance to grow in maturity.

Sources of grief

There are many reasons why grief is a normal life experience. When a person (or group or culture) moves, or expects to move, away from a predictable pattern of living, he or she is confronted with the unknown or the unfamiliar. Few people or organizations can relate to the unknown, the unpredictable or chaos without feeling anxiety, apprehension, or fear.

For example, in case study 4 the sister expresses anxiety: 'I am dreading old age'. Her grief is further intensified by the fact that for most of her life her sense of identity has been derived from her role as a teacher, not primarily from her commitment to religious life. On retirement she suddenly no longer knows *who* she is. In case study 9 groups of former pupils of the schools from which the religious congregation are retiring are bewildered, because they feel that the identity of the schools is integrally dependent on the administrative and teaching presence of members of the congregation. When the latter leave, the identity of the schools—and even of former pupils—will be destroyed. And this causes grief.

The situation of the foreign missionaries as described in case study 6 is worthy of special comment, because unfortunately many missionary groups within the Roman Catholic and Protestant Churches have fallen into the same trap—and some still continue to do so. They refuse to hand over power to local people administratively and pastorally. They deny the reality that the people are more than ready to administer their own affairs and develop their own local theology; they ignore the fact that they are no longer needed. Often the mission-sponsoring organizations have an identity that has come from being needed in foreign lands. Now, once this need has ended, they cannot face the challenge to redefine their purpose in the light of entirely new needs, or simply to cease to exist. They ignore the challenge by *denying* that they are no longer needed.

Grief is the cost we must pay for loving. We can become so attached to some work, group, or person that when separation occurs we feel that something of ourselves has been destroyed. This is how the parishioner in case study 2 felt as he realized that his new parish church did not have his favorite devotional shrines. He had also lost his network of friends who for years had worshipped together and had in need faithfully supported one another. The pain of loneliness now gripped him, for his new parishioners were not interested in offering him the same warm support and companionship.

Stages of grieving

Grief is a process that may at times be characterized by several stages. Though authors differ about the number of the stages involved,[7] the following four stages at least are commonly claimed to occur. In the first stage there is the feeling of numbness, even denial, that loss has occurred. The denial reaction is markedly present among members of the chapter in case study 5, when they are asked to consider the detailed report of their major superior on the future of the province.

In the second stage there is a mixture of strong feelings: a strong pining or nostalgia for what has been lost, a restlessness, despair, an anger that can be directed indiscriminately against friends, God, another culture, superiors, even oneself, as the assumed cause of the grief, then depression. The Maori observer, as described in case study 7, articulates the qualities of this stage of grief. Sometimes the bereaved with a sense of guilt longs for the chance to redress a wrong, fulfill a service, or redeem a relationship with the lost group or individual.

The third stage is marked by a feeling of drifting; the person or group searches reflectively into the past to discover what of value should be carried on into the future and what should be discarded. The temptation for the bereaved at this stage is to cling tenaciously to what has been lost and refuse to face the future.

The fourth stage may be called the recovery or reaggregation period. The bereaved is able to look with some marked detachment at what has been lost; there is the recognition that life must go on and the best of the past must be carried over into the future.

A word of caution about the use of this or any other set of stages of grieving.[8] The process of grieving is extremely complex and no one model of stages can possibly grasp this complexity; a model merely helps us to understand in a very general way what *may* happen to people or organizations in grief. People do not automatically go through these stages; in fact, people can move back and forth from one stage to another, or they may become locked in at any particular stage.

Secondly, a misunderstanding of the models of grieving may lead to the impression that the process of sorrowing can be very neatly controlled according to a clearly defined time period. On the contrary, the process may take months or even years before people become adjusted to their changed circumstances. Some never adjust.

A faulty understanding of the role of denial and depression in the grieving process can also lead to very unfortunate consequences for the people who are grieving and those who try to help them. Denial is 'an unconscious defense mechanism whereby the truth of certain thoughts, feelings, or wishes is disavowed because of its painful or threatening nature'.[9] Denial at times can of course in certain situations be a healthy experience. It can prevent us from receiving the full devastating impact of the shock of loss at one moment, thus giving us the space to begin the process of absorbing what has happened. As T. S. Eliot compassionately writes,

> human kind
> Cannot bear very much reality.[10]

Denial may be neither good nor bad; each case must be evaluated according to the circumstances involved. For example, in case study 3, 'No-nonsense grief', the provincial and superior of the school were refusing to face loss under any circumstances, and demanded that others do the same. The long-term consequences for the teachers were devastating. The denial by the foreign missionaries in case study 6 had become chronic, seriously hindering in consequence the work of localized evangelization. In case study 5, the denial by chapter members of the fact that there had to be a planned withdrawal from some parishes and schools had serious long-term detrimental effects on evangelization in these institutions. When circumstances finally forced the congregation to withdraw, the parishes and schools were left totally unprepared; several parishes are now priestless, with no laity trained to assume leadership, and the schools have been abandoned without any ongoing pastoral care structures being established.

Depression, the feeling of inner emptiness, chaos, or misery, when people feel utterly alone and powerless in their grief, can be an *essential* stage, if grieving is to be a growth-oriented experience. In depression the individual or group has the chance to be stripped of all denial that loss has occurred and that one may have contributed to that loss. This is a process of self-emptying that can be the catalyst of spiritual, psychological, or cultural growth for individuals and communities. Psychologist M. Scott Peck argues that 'Emptiness, depression, and death are analogous because they are the concomitants of the bedrock we must reach if we are to effect change. These stages are basic to human nature and the patterns and rules of human change, whether as individuals or as groups.'[11] He claims that the United States as a nation refuses to admit that the Vietnam war was morally and militarily a total failure, a 'national sin', because it refuses to allow itself to enter into the depression stage. Only if the nation enters into the agony of self-reflection, with all its accompanying doubts and pain, will it admit its mistakes and allow room for national revitalization.[12] The same could be said for Australia and New Zealand about their defeat at the battle of Gallipoli, as described in this chapter.

Summary

The sadness of grief is a consequence of loss or change. And since we live in a world of change, grief is an inevitable and frequent part of daily living. Grieving is not an illness; it becomes a sickness only when groups or individuals fail to confront the experience positively. As Colin Parkes writes, 'Willingness to look at the problems of grief and grieving instead of turning away from them is the key to successful grief work in the sufferer, the helper, the planner, and the research worker'.[13]

Those who are willing to confront the problems of grief must be aware of the contradictory impulses that loss evokes. On the one hand, there is the urge to cling tenaciously to what is lost and that which gave meaning to one's life, even to deny that loss has occurred; on the other hand, there is the need to rebuild a way of life or new relationships in which what was positive from the past is maintained and even revitalized. The ever-present danger is to keep giving way to the first impulse. Then the chance for the bereaved individuals and cultures to re-evaluate the meaning of life and grow in strength is missed.

Unfortunately the acceptance of death or loss, and the need

to grieve over loss, is scarcely recognized in Western cultures. Death is systematically being removed from our consciousness—a form of planned obsolescence. Traditional mourning rituals have been twisted, or new ones invented, to hide death and discourage any form of personal or public grief.[14] In several of the case studies recorded above, people yearned for public and corporate rituals to proclaim that significant losses had occurred, but their leaders did not see the need for these healing rituals. In these rituals, that which is lost is challenged to let go its haunting or suffocating grip on the living; the living are called to face the future supported by what is valuable from the past. In the next chapter I explain more fully why *public* and particularly *corporate* mourning rituals are crucially important and how they should be structured.

Discussion questions

1. What two points in the Introduction and in Chapter 1 do members feel are particularly relevant at present to their group? Why?
2. Are you surprised to read that groups/communities/cultures do experience grief? If so, why?
3. Does the analysis of the stages of grieving fit the experience of the group's members?
4. Have members of the group ever experienced chronic denial in organizations they have been involved with?
5. In this chapter there are ten case studies in which individuals/groups experience grief. What particular case study most appeals to the group? Why? Could individuals or the group provide other examples to illustrate particular points in the chapter?
6. After studying this chapter, do you think it is important for individuals/communities to acknowledge that loss has taken place? If so, why?

References

1. *A Grief Observed* (London: Faber & Faber, 1961), p. 7.
2. See Richard A. Kalish, *Death, Grief, and Caring Relationships* (Monterey, CA: Brooks-Cole, 1983), p. 218; for an overview of the research material on grief and bereavement, see B. Raphael, *The Anatomy of Bereavement* (New York: Basic Books, 1983).
3. *Loss* (New York: Basic Books, 1980), p. 18.

4. See F. Devine, 'Final assault on the Gallipoli myth', *The Australian* (5 February 1990), p. 11.
5. See Merren Parker, *A Time to Grieve* (Auckland: Methuen, 1981), pp. 15–22; see also P. Marris, *Loss and Change* (London: Routledge & Kegan Paul, 1974), pp. 23–42.
6. See R. J. Kastenbaum, 'Death and bereavement in later life' in A. H. Kutscher (ed.), *Death and Bereavement* (Springfield, IL: Charles C. Thomas, 1969), pp. 69–80.
7. See J. R. Averill, 'Grief: its nature and significance', *Psychological Bulletin*, no. 70 (1968), pp. 721–48; E. Kübler-Ross, *On Death and Dying* (New York: Macmillan, 1969); C. M. Parkes, *Bereavement: Studies of Grief in Adult Life* (Harmondsworth, Middx: Penguin, 1986); L. Pincus, *Death in the Family* (New York: Vintage Books; London: Faber & Faber, 1974).
8. See M. A. Simpson, 'Social and psychological aspects of dying' in H. Wass (ed.), *Dying: Facing the Facts* (New York: McGraw-Hill, 1979), pp. 123–25.
9. H. Goldenberg, *Abnormal Psychology: A Social/Community Approach* (Monterey, CA: Brooks-Cole, 1977), p. 586.
10. 'Burnt Norton' in *Four Quartets* (London: Faber & Faber, 1959), p. 14.
11. *The Different Drum: Community-Making and Peace* (London: Rider, 1987), pp. 222f.
12. Ibid., pp. 223f.
13. *Bereavement: Studies of Grief in Adult Life* (Harmondsworth, Middx: Penguin, 1986), p. 213.
14. See P. Ariès, *Western Attitudes toward Death from the Middle Ages to the Present* (Baltimore: Johns Hopkins University Press, 1974), pp. 85–107.

Chapter 2

LETTING GO FOR NEWNESS:
CELEBRATING LOSS

Ring out the grief that saps the mind (Tennyson, *In Memoriam*, cvi, st. 3).

While I was strolling one morning through the small New England village of Onset, I came across this amateurishly painted notice:

> Please understand that we are not asking for a parade, a monument or pity. But we do ask you to remember in your own way the 58,129 Americans who died at the [Vietnam] war. . . . We as individuals and as a nation learned something of human value for having been in S.E. Asia. The sacrifice we maintain was not futile . . .

This is a powerfully poignant plea that the nation admit in *public* or *corporate* ritual that thousands of lives had been lost and that serious military and political mistakes had been made. As noted earlier, the nation, however, still refuses to enter into the public and depressing, but necessary, pain of ritually acknowledging what happened in the war. As long as this refusal continues, the nation will remain trapped in the false belief that the war was a resounding success. Critically important lessons for the nation's future will continue to remain unlearnt and thousands of veterans and their families must continue to sorrow privately, their inner pain and the truth about the nation's guilt ignored.

This privately-erected notice in tiny Onset contains a key lesson of this book: peoples everywhere must collectively admit to cultural or organizational losses, otherwise the past will cling to the living and prevent them from being open to the new. In this chapter I explain the nature of public rituals of grief/healing and how they can be used as agents of creative freedom for society *and* individuals.

Understanding ritual's importance

Ritual is the stylized or repetitive, symbolic use of bodily movement and gesture within a social context, to express and articulate meaning.[1] Ritual action takes place within a social context,
where there is potential or real tension/conflict in social
relations, and is undertaken to resolve or hide it. For example,
according to Japanese custom, when people resolve or hide a
tension/conflict situation between them, they bow to each other
(the equivalent of shaking hands in Western cultures). The
bowing is a gesture of stylized form that at least outwardly
conveys the meaning that harmony in social relationships
exists.

Everday life is filled with ambiguity. It has its inevitable
tensions, potential or actual conflicts, no matter how perfect a
situation may initially appear. A husband and wife know that
no matter how deep their love for each other may be there is
still danger that it will be destroyed, unless they reaffirm this
love from time to time. Hence the importance they place on
the giving of gifts to each other and on the marking of important family anniversaries.

Not surprisingly, therefore, all cultures have rituals surrounding the dramatic, the fear-creating experiences of birth,
marriage, and death, or significant losses of all kinds. These
rituals are generally referred to as *rites of passage*, because they
mark the formal passage of individuals and groups from one
status to another in society—for example, from youth to adult-
hood, from unmarried to married, from life to death. On these
occasions, not just individuals are involved, but whole social
groups are affected, so tension/conflict must be resolved or
hidden to avoid disruption of social relationships.

Some cultures, especially in the Western world, have
developed highly sophisticated rituals of chronic denial in
order to hide the tension that results from loss. But the tension
and sadness cannot always remain hidden, as we see in the
above plea of the Vietnam veterans to American society to put
aside the chronic denial of its defeat in the war. The following
example further illustrates this point.

The Marxist government in Hungary, after crushing the
revolt in 1956, forbade all public mourning over the failure of
the revolt. This suppression of grieving was itself an effort to
impose on the population a ritual of denial; the subversive

memory of the revolt had to be erased from the nation. Thus when the Soviets murdered Imre Nagy, the leader of the abortive revolt, together with other patriots, they secretly disposed of their bodies.

One of the first acts of the new pro-democracy forces in mid-1989 was to exhume the body of Imre Nagy, and the nation was invited to grieve publicly over his death and the sufferings experienced as a nation during and after the abortive revolt. The people were called to assert that the values he and other patriots stood for must form the foundation for a new Hungary. Almost spontaneously a parade of speakers came forward to pledge themselves to strive for the ideals he died for: democracy, neutrality and national independence. Healing involves not only the readiness to grieve, but also the courage to begin again our involvement with life, supported by values and memories of the past.[2]

Insights from traditional cultures

There is much to be learnt from traditional societies about how people and cultures should grieve; frequently in these societies structures are established to facilitate the grieving process for individuals and society itself. People there tend not to hide death or loss because they fear the consequences to society of such deception.

Secondly, the sense of belonging to a corporate person or group that has a person-like existence is extremely strong, so much so that the individual's identity cannot be separated from the context of his or her relationships with the group. Thus, in many traditional cultures if a person is asked his or her name they will first give the name of their tribe or the place where they come from. When the evangelist Matthew wanted to define who Jesus is, he rightly started by listing a long genealogy (Mt 1:1–17).[3] Therefore, any group-oriented person is highly sensitive to the fact that tribes or groups of all kinds can suffer loss and grieve. He or she knows that no matter what their personal feelings may be, they are obliged to join with others and allow the group to grieve.

Public rituals of mourning aim to disentangle from the living that which has been lost—for example, a deceased person or a former social status—and provide the chance for the restoration of a network of social relationships. Yet while that which has been lost must be laid to rest, the positive values it contained need to be integrated into the lives of those deeply affected by the loss.[4] What anthropologist John Middleton says of the Lugbara of Uganda could be said of most traditional cultures:

> A death is more than that of an individual family member: the dead person has also been a member of a lineage which is assumed to be perpetual and a constellation of ties of many kinds was centred upon him. A death disturbs the continuity of the lineage and mortuary rites are performed in order to restore this continuity.[5]

In summary, therefore, there are two major aims in traditional rituals of loss: to separate the dead from the living, and to restore relationships after death has been formally acknowledged. Consequently, there are rites of both separation and reaggregation. In *separation* rites the emphasis is on formally disentangling the deceased from the living—that is, from the immediate family, wider community, and social statuses. At the same time there are also rites that separate those who mourn from the rest of the community; the separation gives the immediately bereaved the space and time to become used to the fact that death has occurred. In the rites of *reaggregation* the dead person is assigned formally to the land of the spirits and the bereaved are ritually returned to the land of the living and given a new set of relationships within the community.[6]

CASE STUDY: NEW ZEALAND MAORI

In New Zealand today the ritual for the dead among Maori remains substantially very much as it has been for centuries. The fact of death is dramatically highlighted. Maori assume that the dead must be properly farewelled and put to rest; if this is not done then the spirit of the dead will haunt the living. Secondly, the bereaved must be comforted and ties of family and social relationships must be renewed; the deep well of what it means to be Maori in today's world must also be tapped, so that all who come to the ritual may be personally and culturally refreshed.[7]

The rites of separation begin as soon as possible after the death. Friends and relatives visit the home of the deceased where women surrounding the body raise the *tangi* (a high-pitched stylized wailing). Prayers are offered and men make the first speeches of farewell to the spirit of the deceased. All the burdens of organizing the funeral are quickly taken over by the extended family of the immediate kin to permit the latter to mourn undisturbed. The body is formally laid out for viewing and is surrounded by photographs of the deceased and his or her ancestors. The immediate kinswomen of the deceased sit beside the casket and rarely leave it until the time for the burial.

Over the next two to three days, mourners (members of the same tribe and friends) arrive most often in groups after sometimes travelling long distances. The visitors, who have some green leaves attached to their clothes, enter the courtyard in front of the body and the chief mourners greet them with renewed wailing and copious tears. Spokespersons for the visitors address the spirit of the deceased, which is thought still to remain close to the body. Stories are told in speeches of welcome and reply about the deceased and his or her virtues are extolled (and quite often, faults and failings are almost brutally listed). The spirit of the deceased is vigorously encouraged through expressions of love and command to go to join its ancestors: 'Farewell! To the threshold of *Matariki* (Pleiades constellation)! Farewell!' The process is repeated over and over again as new visitors arrive, the chief mourners still greeting each group with wails and tears.

At the grave it frequently happens that the clothes of the deceased and his or her most intimate possessions are buried with the corpse. These objects are thought to be dangerous, for they are so impregnated with the sweat and spirit of the deceased; if they remain unburied the spirit of the deceased may still haunt the living. Before the grave is filled an elderly woman cries: 'Go to the belly of the land!' Then members of the family symbolize the break with the deceased by throwing into the grave handfuls of dirt. Thus ends the major ritual whose purpose is to separate the deceased from the living and to encourage the deceased to be at peace with his or her ancestors.

The move to bring back the immediate family of the deceased into the world of the living now begins in earnest. Even before the actual burial ceremony, tribal members are discussing the future of the bereaved spouse and children. Social relationships must be re-established. Directly after the burial a cheerful feast is generally held for all who have attended. The bereaved family meanwhile are formally taken back to their house by elders in order to conduct a rite called 'trample the house'. This rite aims to expel any lingering presence of the spirit of the deceased. An old woman calls out: 'Welcome. . . . Trample in the footsteps of the friend you have lost today!' The mourners are then welcomed to where the feast is taking place with weeping and words like: 'Welcome, the bereaved. Return to your people!'[8]

The rites of separation and reaggregation are formally completed with the unveiling of the headstone on the grave, normally a year after the burial of the deceased. The extended family pay for the stone and often decorate it themselves, sparing no effort to show the dead person that he or she is still remembered and being cared for. The pattern of the ritual is similar, though simpler, to that of the funeral service (*tangi*). A photograph of the deceased takes the place of the body. Prayers are said to ensure that the deceased will now finally lie in peace, satisfied with the memorial that has been constructed in their honor, thus allowing the living to return fully to society without fear of being haunted by the deceased spirit. The widow or widower, since no further obligations remain to the dead person, is declared free to remarry. Social relationships, disrupted by death, are now expected to return to normal; the bereaved corporate person and immediate relatives have completed their rites of mourning.

Occasionally in Western cultures, especially when the loss has particular poignancy, the pattern of separation and reaggregation rites appears, though not with the same sharp clarity evident in traditional cultures. The AIDS Memorial Quilt of San Francisco is a huge tapestry of hand-sewn patches that aims to memorialize the dead and console the living. The quilt, continually growing as more names are added to it, is a metaphor, one quilter says, for placing pieces of lives back together again. Its therapeutic power is said to be much like that of the Vietnam War Memorial in Washington, DC: a collection of names and mementoes that can be seen and touched by the survivors. In other ways also, San Francisco artists have begun to ritualize the disaster. A Candelight Parade is held annually, and a Day of Remembrance is observed on the feast of All Hallows. Such ritual aims to have a public opinion educational value: the problem can be alleviated, it is hoped, if consciousness is raised far enough.[9]

The twofold function of rites of passage

These examples show that genuine rites of passage have legitimizing (or descriptive) and prescriptive qualities. The *legitimizing* function of the ritual is to acknowledge publicly that loss has occurred, and that consequently it is right and necessary for people to grieve/mourn openly that which is lost. When my father died he was accompanied into the parish church by the wailing of Maori women, and this was the sign to all that one of their community had died and that it was quite legitimate to express grief in public.

Rites of passage also *prescribe* how people should feel and what practical steps mourners must take to disentangle themselves from what is lost. They are also told how they are to transfer its memory actively into the present and the future. This function ensures that people do not feel unduly anxious about how to act at crucial and fear-creating points in the life cycle. Chaos is kept under control. This function is clearly realized in Maori death rituals; the deceased is reminded not to interfere in the lives of their family and friends, and the living (individuals and the extended family or tribe) are told what ritual steps they must take to work through their grief successfully.

These twofold functions are in response to needs of the bereaved at three levels: the psychological, mythological and sociological levels.[10] If any of these levels are overlooked, then grief cannot be positively worked through by the bereaved. At the psychological level people require a ritual that culturally permits or encourages them to express fully and openly their feelings of loss (denial, anger, depression, emptiness). People need to see meaning in their loss, so theological or cultural myths are articulated in the ritual that both console and challenge the bereaved to reflect on the purpose of life. For example, for Christians the paschal mystery is the foundational myth and ultimately gives meaning to all who mourn. At the sociological level the bereaved need to feel that their grief is understood and shared by others, and that at the right moment they can return to society and be fully accepted by it (see Figure 2.1).

Grieving: a social drama

The process of grieving is, in anthropologist Victor Turner's terminology, a social drama. We can be helped to understand better how rituals of loss should take place, if Turner's insight into the role of the social drama is better appreciated.

Turner asserts that society is a process, not something static; it is created over and over again out of the effort to resolve the tensions between order and creativity. Integral to this process is the social drama. In the social drama, after a society or a culture experiences a loss, the normal pattern or order of society is temporarily suspended and the group is forced to reflect on its own behavior in the light of its foundational values, even if this means at times the questioning of the relevance of these values. 'In other words', writes Turner, 'dramas induce and contain reflexive processes and generate cultural frames in which flexibility can find a legitimate place.'[11]

A social drama has typically four phases, each of which has its own characteristics and time span: breach, crisis, redressive action, and reintegration (or schism). A *breach* is an underlying breakdown in social relationships, that is, the social status quo is lost; an example of a breach is the Cold War that developed between the East and West after 1945, as it destroyed the East–West alliance relationship that had existed during the years of the Second World War.

A *crisis* is an event resulting from the breach that cannot be ignored; the Berlin blockade by the Soviets is such an occurrence. The crisis phase is 'usually one of these turning points or moments of danger and suspense when a true state of affairs is revealed, when illusions are dispelled and masks torn off or made impossible to don'.[12] Factions or alliances develop to press for this or that strategy to resolve the crisis—some for the return to that which was lost, others for a new set of relationships. If the phase continues, then people are forced to take yet stronger stands based on what they perceive to be moral principles. A war of words can develop.

The third phase, *redressive action*, is often a lengthy and complicated process. The crisis has produced a feeling of

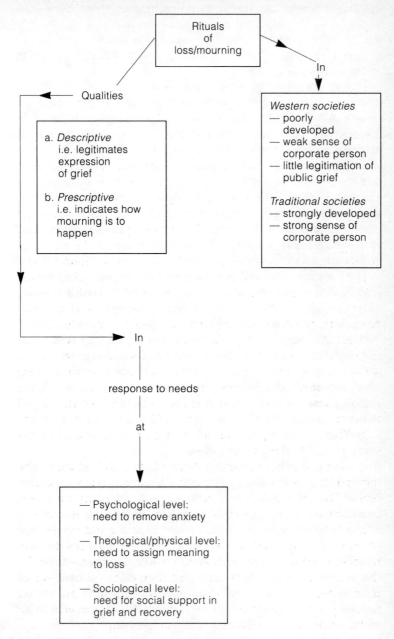

Figure 2.1

chaos, senselessness, or meaninglessness, and this can be a most terrifying experience. People feel the need to discover meaning in what is happening, and to do this they are forced to reflect on fundamental principles or myths that could guide them in resolving the crisis.

In this period of *reflexivity* there is a struggle to resolve the crisis through secular rituals—for example, through the law courts, arbitration, revolution, and war, or through sacred rituals, such as rites of discernment or of mourning. People generally experience considerable pain or emotional turmoil in this phase if their reflection is genuine. They are angered at what has happened and are tempted to deny that loss has occurred. The more they reflect on the foundational values of their group, however, the more they discover that they cannot take refuge in past achievements or ignore the crisis; what is good in the past must be carried forward into the risk-filled future with faith and courage.

The fourth phase, called *reintegration*, is characterized by the parties either resolving their differences with even a heightened sense of unity or breaking apart into *schism*. The Berlin blockade was overcome when the allies, led by the United States, after vocally resisting the Soviets, further reflected on the implications of their commitment to democracy. Loyalty to the principles of democracy led to the concerted and successful effort to break the blockade. Conciliation with the Soviets did not eventuate, but instead there emerged a more deeply rooted schism between the East and West.

Turner focuses particular attention on the tripartite psychosocial stages of the ritual process of the third phase—namely, that of ritual reflexivity (see Figure 2.2). First, there is the *separation* stage, in which there is the temporary breaking away by individuals and society from the predictable pattern of hierarchical roles and statuses of everyday living (called *societas*).

The second stage is *liminality*, the period of reflexivity *par excellence* already referred to above. Ideally this is the time in which people relate to fellow ritual participants and/or to the deity/spirits in, at least symbolically, an undifferentiated ecstatic oneness that is called *communitas*. The purpose of the stripping away of familiar roles or statuses is to allow participants to be open to the influence of creative forces, as represented by creation or regeneration myths. These forces have little chance consciously to affect people in their busy

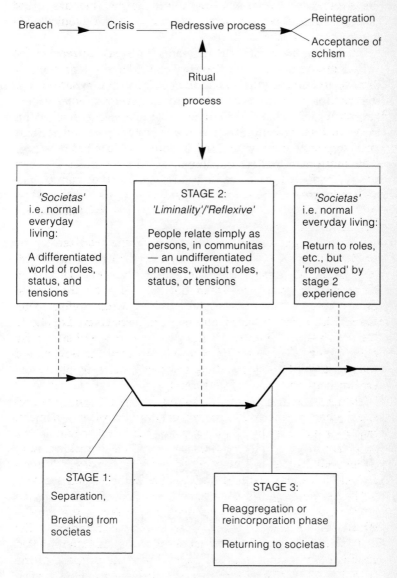

Figure 2.2 Life as a journey (V. Turner's model modified)

day-to-day living. Often the root metaphor in the mythology is death/resurrection; for example, the Christian who unites his own loss with that of Christ's suffering, death, and resurrection will receive the strength to rise to new life.[13] (See Figure 2.3.)

If in the liminality stage participants interiorize, or are reconverted to, the mythology, they feel the urge in passing out of liminality to *recreate* the world according to their experience of the mythology. The status quo, in which key societal values are compromised, will no longer be tolerated. Ideally, the experience of communitas creates a bonding between ritual participants that may endure beyond the liminality stage, enriching post-ritual relationships.

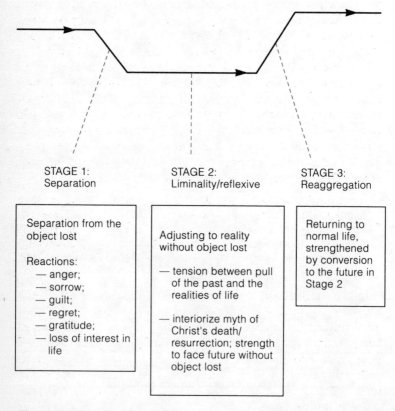

STAGE 1:
Separation

STAGE 2:
Liminality/reflexive

STAGE 3:
Reaggregation

Separation from the object lost

Reactions:
— anger;
— sorrow;
— guilt;
— regret;
— gratitude;
— loss of interest in life

Adjusting to reality without object lost

— tension between pull of the past and the realities of life

— interiorize myth of Christ's death/ resurrection; strength to face future without object lost

Returning to normal life, strengthened by conversion to the future in Stage 2

Figure 2.3 Ritual of loss/grief

In the third stage, in the rites of *reaggregation*, participants move back into the world of statuses or roles (that is, *societas*). This is a difficult stage because ritual participants are tempted, in the face of the busyness and pressures of everyday life, to go back on the commitments generated in the stage of liminality. We look now at two case studies of mourning that illustrate this theory; the examples have a pattern somewhat akin to that normally found in traditional cultures.

CASE STUDIES

1. The loss of a post office

The New Zealand government recently decided that many post offices serving small communities should be closed because they had become too costly to maintain. This decision marked the breach phase in the social drama affecting remote townships. Residents recognized, as happened for example in the small town of Eketahuna, that the normally peaceful relationships with the government were in danger of fracturing.

The crisis point came for the residents of Eketahuna when they heard that they were to lose *their* post office. They joined together in lengthy discussions with a unity never before seen in the town, and they decided to send a delegation to ask the government to reconsider the closure decision; however, this was unsuccessful. In the third phase, reflexivity, they pondered in depth the reasons why they should not lose the post office. One resident articulated the commonly held views:

> Rural districts are being killed off and the people living in them rejected. This is not what New Zealand life is all about; after all, our pioneers cared for one another and especially for the poor. If we lose our post office we will lose our identity as a community, we will cease to be a town, we no longer will have a name. And that is poverty.

In their reflections together the people rediscovered that in the New Zealand creation mythology the rights of the marginalized and poor must be respected. They saw themselves as being in danger of becoming nationally marginalized without a post office and this gave them the energy and legitimacy to act. And act they did. Young and old, professional and unskilled people, linked arms and surrounded the small post office to prevent the removal of the post boxes.

The government did not change its decision. Nor did the

residents bow to government pressure to accept financial viability as *the* measure for having the services of a post office. A schism in a sense developed between the townspeople and the government, one that would affect how the residents of the town would vote in the next national elections. Yet, though this 'schism' emerged, most townspeople recognized that ultimately they could not change the government's decision. Because they had worked and reflected together on the project, they had discovered new resources as a group; they were now prepared to use this energy for new projects for the town. The social drama and the mourning ritual had been a positive experience.

2. Closing a formation house

A formation house for religious sisters that had existed for over 100 years was threatened with closure, because of a dramatic decline over the previous three years in the number of candidates entering the training program. For the province this caused the first phase of a social drama, a *breach*, that is, a breakdown of a predictable behavior pattern. Up to three years previously the formation house had been receiving ten or more candidates a year, but for the subsequent two years the numbers had dropped to one per year. The previous year no one applied to enter the congregation.

The *crisis* phase developed when the problem of financially maintaining a large almost empty house could no longer be ignored. Opposing factions emerged; some denied that any problem existed at all, others sought to confront the province with the realities of the loss. A powerful lobby demanded that under no circumstances should the house be sold, as the history of the province and its own identity were so intimately linked with the house. 'If the house is sold', complained one religious, 'then we will disintegrate as a province. No longer will we have any roots!' Other factions loudly pushed for selling the house and establishing the formation program in a smaller building well adapted to a process of formation totally different from that of the past. One person summarized the feeling of several:

> As long as we keep this huge empty house we will be haunted by memories of an older, out-of-date method of formation and this will continue to dictate how we form our small numbers of religious today. The house is physically shaped by a model of

religious life that is not Vatican II. If we continue to hold on to it, it will insidiously harm our formation process. We must admit that the old will no longer work.

The official congregational leaders—the provincial and her council—recognized that the crisis had to be resolved. Representatives of the major factions were selected and asked to research into the future of formation and into the relevance of the present formation house. They were advised not just to gather information, but also to use a discernment process as a way of finally reflecting on the material they had gathered. On the completion of several months of research, the group having decided to spend a week in a quasi-retreat atmosphere, they began with a day of silence in private prayer. This marked the *separation* stage and the entrance into the liminal phase in which they sought in faith and prayer to ponder together the findings of their research. The ultimate criterion for their reflections became: What is the Holy Spirit asking of us? Over the next few days each individual, no matter what their private views may have been, was asked first to argue in favor of a particular option, then to argue against the same option. The process was repeated for each option. One individual summarized what happened to herself and to the group:

> I entered the process with clear ideas about what should be done with the formation house. But, when I was asked to come up with contrary arguments, I found myself quite lost. Emotionally it was tough being pressured to present opposing arguments and to let go of my strongly held views even if it was only for the sake of the process. Soon I felt quite lost. The rigidity with which I had held on to my personal views about formation began to seem totally out of place.
>
> At times I felt angry without quite knowing why, sometimes I yearned for the old days when formation seemed simpler and neatly structured. Others said they felt the same. We began to feel closer to the Lord in Gethsemane and this emerged in our shared prayer over the days. Like the Lord we had to let go of our views and ask the Father that we respond to his will. This meant going back to basic questions like: 'What is religious life?' 'What are the formation implications of the answer to this question?' Now the really tough work took place, yet we felt united as we had never been before.
>
> Finally, we all agreed that the house had to be sold and that we should not just move to a small formation house, but that the whole formation process should change in light of the commitment

to the world that Vatican II asked of us. We began to feel sad about our recommendation that the old formation house should go. We decided then to have a liturgy to farewell it from our lives and a good part of the prayer session was spent in sitting around telling stories—some funny, some not so—about our own experiences in the house.

The administration accepted our recommendation to close the house, but the problem was now to help the province understand. This was not easy—in fact, it is still hard, even though the house has gone and a new formation process is in place. How can I ever explain to people the depth of unity we experienced as a team when working through the process of discernment! In explaining the decision to withdraw from the house, we as a team visited other houses and we held liturgies of mourning like we had had as a team. These were well accepted and eased the situation immensely. But some groups in the province still do not accept the decision adopted by the provincial administration. I feel in their hearts they are drifting away from the province. It takes a long time for hurts to disappear—doesn't it?

The commentary illustrates what is apt to happen in the liminality process: the movement from 'I' to 'we' (communitas), the feeling of chaos or of deep loss where once certainty existed, the urge to rediscover the creation myth or root metaphor of the group, the creative energy that emerges if the group is honestly open to the experience, the difficulties of explaining the decision to the non-participants (the challenge of the reintegration stage), the failure of some in the province to accept the administration's decision ('schism'). The commentator is describing a dual movement of letting go. First, each participant is challenged to let go of her view when it is seen to diverge from what the Lord wishes; secondly, the group must learn to let go of its own sense of security in order to risk sharing its conclusions with outsiders. The temptation is for the group, when faced with the reintegration phase, to withdraw into the comfort of its own happy memories.

Summary

Unless we understand and celebrate death we cannot opt for life. The anxiety, pain, anger, fear, and depression that significant loss evokes in us as individuals and groups must be expressed/celebrated, otherwise we cannot embrace the future with freshness and creativity. Traditional cultures can teach us how to celebrate death in a socially dramatic and healthy way: the group must acknowledge loss and grieve over it, not just individuals; rituals of grieving must be so structured that public expressions of grief are permissible, and even expected.

In the following chapter we see why in Western societies we commonly deny the reality of death. Gospel communities must be conscious of the subtle influence of this cultural denial on themselves and deliberately aim to build structures that help them to acknowledge, and positively work through, significant loss in their lives.

Discussion questions

1. How would you explain to people who are not aware of the need for cultures/communities to grieve, why rituals of public/corporate mourning are of critical importance?

2. Does the analysis of life as a social drama fit your own experience? Could members of the group share examples?

3. Has your group/community ever constructed a ritual of mourning because of some loss it has experienced? How would you go about constructing such a ritual? What points should you particularly have in mind?

References

1. See R. Bocock, *Ritual in Industrial Society: A Sociological Analysis of Ritualism in Modern England* (London: George Allen & Unwin, 1974), pp. 35–59.
2. See S. Seibert and N. Meyer, 'Hero's resurrection', *The Bulletin* (Australia) (27 June 1989), pp. 68f.
3. See G. A. Arbuckle, *Earthing the Gospel: An Inculturation Handbook for Pastoral Workers* (London: Geoffrey Chapman, 1990), p. 46.
4. See P. Marris, *Loss and Change* (London: Routledge & Kegan Paul, 1974), p. 31.
5. 'Lugbara death' in M. Bloch and J. Parry (eds), *Death and the Regeneration of Life* (Cambridge, UK: Cambridge University Press, 1982), p. 134; see also R. Huntington and P. Metcalf, *Celebrations of Death: The Anthropology of Mortuary Ritual* (Cambridge, UK: Cambridge University Press, 1979), pp. 23–118.
6. J. Goody, *Death, Property and the Ancestors* (London: Tavistock, 1962), p. 46.

7. See H. Dansey, 'A view of death' in M. King (ed.), *Te Ao Hurihuri: The World Moves On* (Wellington: Hicks Smith, 1975).
8. See J. Metge, *The Maoris of New Zealand Rautahi* (London: Routledge & Kegan Paul, 1976), pp. 261–64; A. Salmond, *Hui: A Study of Maori Ceremonial Gatherings* (Wellington: A. H. & A. W. Reed, 1975), pp. 180–93; T. Rangi Hiroa, *The Coming of the Maori* (Wellington: Whitcombe and Tombs, 1977), pp. 414–30. Readers who are particularly interested in feeling the power of death as an affirmation of life in Maori culture are encouraged to read *Tangi*, a poetic drama in prose by Witi Ihimaera (Auckland: Heinemann Reed, 1989).
9. *The Economist* (6 May 1989), p. 104.
10. See I. Ainsworth-Smith and P. Speck, *Letting Go: Caring for the Dying and the Bereaved* (London: SPCK, 1982), p. 62.
11. *From Ritual to Theatre: The Human Seriousness of Play* (New York: Performing Arts Journal Publications, 1982), p. 92.
12. V. Turner, *On the Edge of the Bush: Anthropology as Experience* (Tucson: University of Arizona Press, 1985), p. 215.
13. See G. A. Arbuckle, *Strategies for Growth in Religious Life* (New York: Alba House, 1986), pp. 185–201.

Chapter 3

DENYING LOSS IN
WESTERN CULTURES

[Grieving in the West] is treated as if it were a weakness, a self-indulgence, a reprehensible bad habit instead of a psychological necessity (G. Gorer).[1]

Neither the individual nor the community is strong enough to recognize the existence of death (P. Ariès).[2]

In the preceding chapter I said that significant loss like death gives a unique chance for specialized ritual and symbolic representation. The most common underlying theme in such ritual should be that order, represented by life, becomes death or disorder. Cosmos is replaced by chaos. The purpose of a ritual of grieving or mourning is the restoration of order, after the chaos is recognized and accepted, but this process can take so long in some traditional cultures that a whole generation can pass before it is ended.

Today, however, most Western cultures simply do not prescribe or foster any healthy mourning rituals whatsoever. The way of death is a finely manipulated use of silence, denial, or avoidance of the depressing chaos experience that accompanies it. Death is now a logistical problem for the systems analysts who are to be concerned with it: doctors, funeral directors, clergymen, lawyers. It is being systematically removed from our consciousness—a form of planned obsolescence.[3]

Naturally grief is something not to be talked about, and only rarely and publicly displayed. Franklin D. Roosevelt was possibly one of the last notable figures who openly grieved when his mother died, because he wore a black armband, a custom that has now almost totally disappeared.[4] Denial, writes Charles Jackson, 'has become an art form and . . . dying is [presented] as an alien unnatural humiliation'.[5] And Philippe Ariès, a noted authority on this topic, writes of this denial that 'It is above all essential that society . . . notice to the least possible degree that death has occurred. . . . If a ceremony still marks the departure, it must remain discreet and must avoid emotion.'[6]

This is a thoroughly pathetic and frightening picture of a death-denying society, for just as we seek to deny physical death, so also we are apt to ignore all kinds of painful personal and social loss. We have developed a pervasive mythology in which success is the hallmark of Western identity and failure or loss has no place in it. Not surprisingly, therefore, the paschal mystery finds little welcome or understanding within our contemporary Western world.

Remember that this death-denying culture can be alive within us, without our being at all aware it is influencing our attitudes and actions. In order to develop a spirituality of refounding within this unsupportive cultural atmosphere, we must know thoroughly what we are culturally up against. Hence, I now describe a typical North American funeral in order to illustrate the ways in which the culture expresses its rituals of denial. The rituals of other Western nations differ in details, but there is the same underlying mythology of denial. I then suggest several reasons why the mythology of denial has developed so strongly.

CASE STUDY: THE AMERICAN WAY OF DEATH

Over a three-month period in 1986 in one American city, I attended several funeral rituals; the pattern described below is similar to that presented by other observers.[7]

Generally, death rituals are highly expensive and people feel considerable social pressure to spend lavishly. Mourners are discouraged from expressing any emotion; somber restraint is an esteemed virtue. At a member's death, the family is removed from all care and preparation of the deceased for burial; embalming and grooming experts ensure that all signs of death are removed by carefully hiding scars, replacing missing limbs with plaster substitutes, and thin and sickly bodies are made healthy-looking. 'Doesn't he look good', said one mourner. 'He looks happy and far better than in life! It makes me feel good to see him like this.'

Brief times for mourners to view the body are set and also how they are to go about this ceremony is carefully monitored. Visitors looked ill-at-ease at the funerals I witnessed; on entering the viewing parlor they would try to avoid either the open casket or/and the bereaved family. Any conversation tended to be brief and sprinkled with euphemisms to avoid direct reference to the taboo topic of death. The bereaved family or spouse would be consoled with words that discouraged any form of open grief, as these representative comments indicate:

'You know, dear, you must feel happy for he is asleep, as you can see!'

'God has taken him to himself. You should feel happy and not cry!'

'He wants you to be strong and immediately get back to work. He would be quite unhappy if you stopped to think about him and kept on crying.'

'I think you are bearing up marvelously well. Even your clothes are bright. That is good, for you need to be joyful and it helps the family. And she would have wanted you to be like this.'

'I do like the way you are colorfully dressed. I can't stand the old style of mourning—those black clothes the Italians wear remind me of, well . . . you know!'

Following the burial (or cremation) ceremonies, those who attend the funeral are generally invited by the immediate family or mourners to a meal, either at their home or at a restaurant. Those who accept do not stay longer than is strictly necessary. There is the same uneasiness as was seen at the funeral parlor, and there is the constant effort to conduct conversation with as little reference as is possible to the fact that someone has just been buried. Again there are the same attempts to encourage a false joy and an ongoing denial in the bereaved. 'Go out and enjoy yourself. Go for a trip. She would want you to. I did, and I forgot all about what had happened. Just go out and live life! Forget the past, beginning from today.'

In terms of ritual mourning explained in the previous chapter, the funeral rituals I attended opted to stress the need for the bereaved to be aggregated as quickly as possible back into ordinary living, but with the minimum, if any, reference to the separation of the deceased from the living and the living from the dead. Only one thing was important: make sure the deceased are physically disposed of with as much discreet haste as is socially acceptable, then ignore that there has been death, and get back to a busy life immediately.

As regards Turner's social drama model, these Western rituals of death acknowledge the breach and crisis phases, but lightly trip over or ignore the reflexive, ritual phase. That is, the separation and liminality stages of the ritual process are skillfully avoided. The impact of death or significant loss on the bereaved person and the subculture(s) (for example, the deceased's employing organization, recreational clubs) to which the deceased and his or her family belonged, is ignored. The cultural imperative is: let no grief be publicly shown and every effort must be made by the bereaved individual, friends, and subculture(s) to reintegrate into life as though nothing had happened. The whole range of grief reactions—pining, numbness, anger, despair, guilt, the struggles to take the experience of the past into the future—are to be ignored, repressed, or permitted only the briefest possible acknowledgment. (See Figure 3.1.)

The question remains: Why in Western cultures today do we frequently strive so vigorously (and expensively) to camouflage or repress death from our personal and public awareness? The question can be put in another way: Why do our cultures deprive us of our own deaths and of the right to mourn others

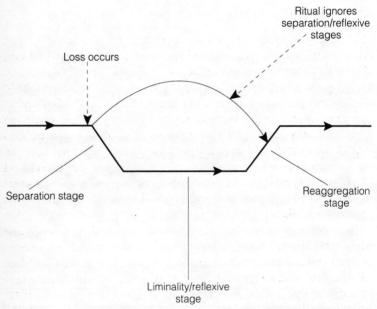

Figure 3.1 Ritual of loss denial: avoiding separation/liminality/ reflexive stages

who die? I can identify eight interrelating answers to these questions:

1. Lack of visibility of death

Within many parts of the Third World death is a highly visible reality. For example, one day after I had finished celebrating the Eucharist in a Manila slum (about 7,000 people), I was asked to bless a small baby that had just died; within one hour I had blessed a further four.

Death in the First World, on the other hand, is rarely so visible. The average life expectancy is around 75 years, so increasingly it is only the elderly who do the dying. Almost no one dies of hunger or infectious diseases (with the growing exception of AIDS sufferers); thus people often reach middle age before anyone they know well dies. Death for us in its personally visible form has become a distant reality, an abstraction—the kind of death that one reads about or sees safely presented on the television.[8]

2. The privatization of death

In the past, people generally were nursed and died within their own homes, surrounded by their families. In medieval Europe, people were normally expected to sense themselves, or they were told of, their approaching death. They would begin the process of preparing themselves for it. The dying person was on center stage, participating in prayers, receiving relatives and friends, forgiving enemies, giving instructions about what should happen after their death. In brief, people were culturally encouraged to make themselves the masters of their own dying process, and their relatives and friends were expected to begin the grieving process, even before the actual death took place.

The contemporary scene in today's hospital is often quite different. Hospitals are to keep people alive; death is in a sense a mark of failure, even more so as death is seen to be a problem of medical engineering. The patient becomes increasingly a passive agent in his or her own death, a 'puppet' in a 'play' in which the principal actors are the medical staffs and the relatives of the sick or dying person. Doctors and family members hesitate to tell the person that death is imminent or possible. They fear to hurt the sensitivities, or lower the morale, of the suffering person, who daily becomes more and more like a lonely child, rather than an adult involved in the most important process of his or her life. Sometimes the services of religious ministers are discouraged lest they disturb the peace of the patient or get in the way of the hospital staff.

The dying person's family and friends become increasingly isolated, strained, and alienated from the patient. They are apt to feel, as they surround the dying person's bed, that they are trespassing on foreign territory—that is, in an institution that is primarily concerned with healing the sick. Dying and death after all are really signs of institutional failure, and inevitably many hospital staff find this a difficult fact to adjust to. David Dempsey claims 'The essence of the family's game is pretense. . . . Appearances are kept up; there is much small talk and forced cheerfulness while the basic feelings, the things that cry out in the heart, go unsaid.'[9]

3. Individualism undermines corporate responsibility

In our dying moments we can pay the price of belonging to a culture in which individualism is an esteemed virtue. That shrewd observer of North American life, Alexis de Tocqueville, noted last century—as something already emerging—the problems of individualism, loneliness, and alienation.[10] The more individualism is pushed, the more the bonds binding people to the group and the common good are weakened. Hence, Robert Bellah could conclude, with deepening sorrow, that as the result of the overstress on individualism, 'marriage, friendship, job . . . church are dispensable, if these don't meet my needs'.[11] A culture of individualism has lost the sense of corporateness and thus the need to grieve the loss of its members. John Donne's famous comment that 'Any man's death diminishes me, because I am involved in Mankind' has little meaning left in a culture of individualism.

4. Commercialization of death

The occupation of undertaking, particularly in North America, has become very big business indeed, largely by transforming the ritual and symbolism of death to conform with the ethic of the consumer society. Financial profit, argues Jessica Mitford, powerfully motivates the industry to continue to hide the painful reality of death from bereaved people.

Whereas once relatives prepared the body of the deceased, this is no longer the case. People are spared the 'dirtiness' of death, as is evident in the terminology used to soften its stark reality. For example, the 'loved one', who has been facially restored to 'robust good health', is laid out for viewing in the 'slumber' or 'reposing' room. Titles like 'funeral director' or 'mortician' are now substitutes for undertaker, 'caskets' for coffins, 'coaches' for hearses. Anything that is thought to convey morbidity or death is taboo.[12] Now even grief therapy has become commercialized by the undertaking business; the bereaved are offered costly sessions on how to work through their grief.

The covering-up of loss throughout society in general has become a sad form of art. William Lutz recently invented the term 'doublespeak' to describe this corruption of language; the word connotes a very conscious use of language as a weapon or tool by those in power to achieve their ends at the expense of others. Through doublespeak, those who are powerful aim to hide for their advantage the reality of pain and loss in all areas of life. People who are sacked in doublespeak are 'dehired' or 'selected out' by firms that are having 'workforce adjustments'; when Chrysler closed a plant, it 'initiated a career alternative enhancement program' and some 5,000 employees lost their jobs. Patients don't experience pain, just 'discomfort'.[13]

5. The inner urge to deny death

Novelist Leo Tolstoy's fictional Ivan Ilych says at one point: 'It cannot be that I ought to die. That would be too terrible.'[14] This is a common contemporary reaction to death. Pulitzer prize-winner Ernest Becker believes that this evasion of death is the result of a deeply rooted in-built denial of death: 'The idea of death, the fear of it, haunts the human animal like nothing else; it is a mainspring of human activity . . . activity designed largely to avoid the fatality of death, to overcome it by denying in some way that it is the final testing of man.'[15] The cultural pressures to camouflage death merely reinforce this inner denial imperative.

Becker's insight is not entirely new, because many a

philosopher has grappled with how to deny death or evade the fear of it. The ancient Greek philsopher Epicurus articulated a way in which he thought he could avoid the fear of death: 'Death is nothing to us; for as long as we are, death is not here; and when death is here, we no longer are. Therefore it is nothing to the living or the dead.'[16] The Christian apologist Blaise Pascal, while reflecting on the seventeenth-century world of his day, could have been describing the contemporary Western denial of death when he wrote:

> Notwithstanding [the] miseries he wants to be happy, and only to be happy, and cannot wish not to be happy, but how is he to set about it? In order to make a good job of it, he would have to make himself immortal, but since he is unable to do so, he tries to stop thinking about it. Since they are unable to cure death, misery, ignorance, men imagine that they can find happiness by not thinking about such things.[17]

The existentialist philsopher Jean-Paul Sartre, whose influence on Western thinking was especially powerful in the 1950s and 1960s, based his attitude to death on the power and primacy of the act of human freedom, whereby the 'stranger death' is absolutely ignored and despised. He believes that the human person can and should subordinate death to such a degree that one can forget the reality and anxiety of death.[18] The moment of death, he argues, is almost always a question of chance. It can never be rightly chosen. It leaves us with tasks uncompleted and potentials undeveloped.

Martin Heidegger, Sartre's contemporary, feels that the anticipation and acceptance of death may well be positive, if they are incentives to face up to the truth of one's life in all its bleaknesses. Sartre, while agreeing in part with Heidegger, nonetheless asserts that the constant appearance of chance at the heart of 'my projects cannot be apprehended as my possibility but, on the contrary, as the nihilation of all my possibilities. . . . Thus death is never that which gives life its meanings; it is, on the contrary, that which on principle removes all meaning from life.'[19] A rather bleak approach to the value of death!

6. The impact of secularism

The Christian view of the after-life has taken a severe beating over the last century, leaving people uncertain about what lies after death. Death is a puzzle. It no longer has a comprehensible meaning, so that the way to avoid being troubled by uncertainty is to deny death and whatever is related to it.

Alexis de Tocqueville could already see the impact of secularism within the emerging American culture of the last century. Americans, he claimed, are highly practical people and possess an enormous optimism about their human ability to know and do anything. They 'readily conclude', he writes, 'that everything in the world can be explained, and that nothing in it transcends the limits of the understanding. Thus they fall to denying what they cannot comprehend.'[20] The weakening of a vigorous belief in an after-life has led inevitably to the decline of public rituals that unambiguously assert the realities of death and the world that follows.

During the period of the Revolution of Expressive Disorder in the 1960s, the entire Western world experienced dramatic changes in assumptions and accepted customs which form the cultural roots of the everyday lives of ordinary people. The social upheaval, one of the speediest and most dramatic in recorded history, started out as a form of cultural revolution among a small group of radicals, and finished by changing some of the most profound ways of acting and beliefs in the Western world. It was a movement against tradition, an opting for the present or for immediacy of experience and self-fulfillment. Traditional or institutional religion took a severe battering. The entire movement reinforced the existing denial of death: ignore the fear of death and death itself and simply experience life in the present.

The immediate causes of the Expressive Revolution are many and complex; for example, the rising demand from minority groups for human rights, the chaos of American involvement in the Vietnam war.[21] In addition, the rapid expansion of higher education, which was followed by an economic recession and unemployment among graduates who had started their studies with high expectations of employment, provided a mass of young graduates and teachers with ample time on their hands for discussion and action.

Given these circumstances it was not at all surprising that

in the 1960s the philosophy of Herbert Marcuse became so immensely popular. He was aware of the fact that it would have been possible for all Western nations to have provided well-established free health services, yet wealth was being diverted for the manufacture of armaments, or for the production of thirty different kinds of similar washing powder, even though one brand would have been enough. He saw this as oppressive, and considered the working classes had been manipulated into providing the labor to maintain such shocking priorities. Since the working classes could not revolt against this oppression, then, argued Marcuse, an elderly German refugee teaching at the University of California, people such as the intellectuals, students and minority groups could unite to overthrow the intolerably repressive culture of false consumerism and war. In Marcuse, the dissatisfied intellectuals of the 1960s found a powerful leader to inspire them. He was able to articulate in words just what they felt and wanted to do.[22]

For Marcuse, the human organism develops in consequence of two fundamental instincts: the life instinct (sexuality, Eros) and the death instinct (the destructive instinct). The life instinct struggles to bind living substance into more and more stable units, but the death instinct urges a return to the condition before birth, the state of inorganic matter. This death instinct fosters in society a repressive atmosphere of work, action without purpose and guilt, and increasingly stifles the life instinct. This process must be reversed in order to allow the life instinct to come to the fore and the death instinct to fade into a state where it no longer causes tension and anxiety. When this happens a new ideal people emerges, incapable of war, violence of all kinds, and working in a new collectivity that would bring art and technology together in unity.[23]

7. *The denial of aging*

The emphasis in the Western world is on looking, feeling, and acting young. One dare not become or look old for then one would have to face the reality of death![24] This point is dramatically made by a British pop group in the lyrics of 'My Generation', a record released in late 1965; the singer several times expresses the hope that he will die before he becomes old. As though to emphasize the point that old age is something to be dreaded as a horrible evil, the music of the record does not fade away, but tears itself to pieces in a lengthy and painful cacophony.

8. The 'pornography' of death

Anthropologist Geoffrey Gorer speaks of the 'pornography' of death. By this he means that it is not to be mentioned publicly; it is to be dealt with only as a private fantasy. He notes that we are acquainted with the impersonal, 'phony phenomenon' of death on television and that we live in a society conditioned to regard death and mourning as strictly private issues. Consequently, people react to the abstract idea of death with a kind of indifference that would have been out of place in earlier times. Confronted with death as a personal crisis, we seem able to do little but escape squeamishly into euphemism.[25]

9. The theological bias against the incarnation

The heresy of Docetism, which asserts that Christ had only an apparent body, plagued the early Church, but, as Karl Rahner writes, it is still very much alive today: 'in the ordinary religious life of the Christian, Christ finds a place only as God'.[26] Hence, Christ did not suffer nor did he die. He only appeared to suffer and die.

The truth is of course that it is only through the incarnation in which God became one of us that our own sufferings and deaths have meaning. The more we acknowledge our weaknesses and our need of the Lord, the more we become united with Christ suffering and rising: 'For the suffering he himself passed through while being put to the test enables him to help others when they are being put to the test' (Heb 2:18). If he did not suffer or die, then there is no reason for us to acknowledge our own mortality; it is something better denied, for it is too humanly burdensome to be reminded of it.

Reactions to the denial of loss

The culture of denial has over the years stimulated some trenchant criticisms. Evelyn Waugh wrote his cutting satire on the American way of death after a visit in 1947 to a monstrously garish rococo cemetery in Hollywood.[27] Reflecting on what he saw, he described the soulless, immature refusal to acknowledge the reality of death:

> Even the names given to their various sections—Eventide, Babyland, Graceland, Inspiration Slope, Slumberland, Sweet Memories . . . are none of them suggestive of the graveyard. . . . Forest Lawn has consciously turned its back on 'the old customs of Death', and grim traditional alternatives of Heaven and Hell, and promises immediately happiness for all its inmates.[28]

The novel is boldly shocking from beginning to end. No distinctions are made between the funeral rites for animals and those for human beings. Dennis Barlow, the main character, offers advice to a would-be customer about the burial possibilities for a Sealyham terrier: 'And the religious rites? We have a pastor who is always pleased to assist. . . . Our grade A service includes several unique features. At the moment of committal, a white dove, symbolizing the deceased's soul, is liberated over the crematorium.'[29] In the absence of the spiritual dimension in life, the preservation of the human or the body of a pet animal at Forest Lawn Memorial Park seems almost a guarantee of immortality. The novel concludes with a macabre adaptation of the custom whereby a bereaved pet-owner receives a card on the anniversary of the pet's death with the reassuring comment: 'Your little Aimee is wagging her tail in Heaven tonight'.[30] Cyril Connolly summarizes the novel's overall aim: 'In its attitude to death, and to death's stand-in, failure, Mr Waugh exposes a materialistic society at its weakest spot, as would Swift and Donne were they alive today'.[31]

Jessica Mitford highlights the financial profit motive as a significant factor in the emergence of rituals of death in the United States. Of the status symbols in an affluent society, structured 'to trap the unwary consumer at every turn', about 'the most irrational and weirdest of the lot, lying in ambush for all of us at the end of the road' is 'the modern American funeral'.[32]

James J. Farrell emphasizes in his study of the evolution of funeral customs in the United States that the sweeping cultural changes, for example, through urbanization, industrialization and professionalization, between 1830 and 1920 inevitably affected American beliefs and behavior about death. Funerals, he writes, have become custom-made in the same way as automobiles are, and the price that is paid is the loss of our own personality: 'By our passive role in directing our funerals, we have transformed an important rite of personal passage into an impersonal rite of passivity. . . . Keeping death out of mind cuts people off from an important fact of their physical, mental, and spiritual existence.'[33]

Death has become a somewhat more popular topic for discussion as a consequence of the writings of people like Elisabeth Kübler-Ross, who sees herself as 'a catalyst, trying to bring to our awareness that we can only truly live and enjoy and appreciate life if we realize at all times that we are finite'.[34] Her insights encourage a healthy rethinking of death and dying. She hopes that we will see the dying as teachers and she has outlined the stages through which people can cope with the knowledge of imminent death. She encourages the dying patient to break the cultural taboo of talking about death by sharing the experience of dying with family and friends.[35]

This more positive approach to death, however, has at times negative side-effects. James Farrell claims that in many ways the modern concern for death 'is only a mutation of the dying of death'. It arises out of 'the therapeutic conviction that we can master what we can touch or talk about'. It reassures us, he says, 'that death should not be miraculous or mysterious'.[36]

Summary

Every culture contains values enshrined in ritual that set out how its members are to relate to the loss of loved ones. This ritual is the model for how individuals and groups are to relate to other forms of loss.

We Christians, especially in the Western world, who struggle to articulate and live out a spirituality of letting go, are at a distinct disadvantage. We live in death-denying cultures. We cosmetically hide the reality of death, even encourage drive-in viewing windows in funeral parlors so that death is given a mere passing glance, use euphemistic language about death, isolate the dying from the living, and reduce them to the level of a technological problem. This is tragic for an experience of significant loss should mean both an end and transition to a new period of creative action, 'both terror and liberation, both something violent and something maturing from within, something happening to us but also something we ourselves perform'.[37]

In subsequent chapters we see how important it is for Christians to foster beliefs and rituals that run counter to cultures that deny loss and the need to mourn. In fact, one of the most dominant themes in both the Old and New Testaments is that of the need to grieve and mourn.

Discussion questions

1. Does the group agree with this chapter's thesis that our Western cultures strongly deny death? If you agree, can you suggest examples not included in the chapter to illustrate the thesis?

2. Let each member of the group take a copy of a daily newspaper. What values do the advertisements project? Are they saying anything about loss or grief? Share your findings with the group.

3. Are there personal experiences of loss that individual members and/or the group have never acknowledged? If so, why? (I suggest that members of the group may prefer to ponder this question alone, without rushing, and in a prayerful atmosphere. *If* they wish, they may then like to share their answers or stories with the group.)

4. Have members of the group ever attended the deathbed of a friend? Did this experience teach them any important lessons?

References

1. *Death, Grief and Mourning in Contemporary Britain* (New York: Doubleday, 1965), p. 85.
2. *The Hour of our Death* (New York: Vintage Books, 1982), p. 614.
3. See R. W. Doss, *The Last Enemy: A Christian Understanding of Death* (New York: Harper & Row, 1974), p. 1.
4. See R. W. Bailey, *The Minister and Grief* (New York: Hawthorn Books, 1976), pp. 80f.
5. In C. O. Jackson (ed.), *Passing: The Vision of Death in America* (Westport: Greenwood Press, 1977), p. 242.
6. *Western Attitudes towards Death: From the Middle Ages to the Present* (London: Johns Hopkins University Press, 1974), p. 90.
7. See D. Dempsey, *The Way We Die: An Investigation of Death and Dying in America Today* (New York: McGraw-Hill, 1975), pp. 167–73; T. P. O'Brien, 'Death, the final passage: a case study in American mortuary custom' in

C. P. Kottak (ed.), *Researching American Culture* (Ann Arbor: University of Michigan Press, 1982), pp. 171–9; T. A. Rando, *Grief, Dying, and Death: Clinical Interventions for Caregivers* (Campaign, IL: Research Press, 1984), pp. 2–9.

8. See *Death and the Hereafter* (Brussels: Pro Mundi, 1985), Dossier no. 31, pp. 2–4; N. Elias, *The Loneliness of the Dying* (Oxford: Basil Blackwell, 1985), *passim*.

9. Dempsey, *The Way We Die*, op. cit., p. 81; see also R. Huntington and P. Metcalf, *Celebrations of Death: The Anthropology of Mortuary Ritual* (Cambridge, UK: Cambridge University Press, 1979), pp. 194ff.

10. See Alexis de Tocqueville, *Democracy in America*, ed. P. Bradley (New York: Alfred A. Knopf, 1953), II, p. 98.

11. 'Religion and power in America today', *Commonweal* (3 December 1982), p. 652.

12. See J. Mitford, *The American Way of Death* (New York: Simon & Schuster, 1963), pp. 18f. and *passim*; Doss, *The Last Enemy*, op. cit., pp. 8f.

13. See *The Dominion* (New Zealand) (26 October 1989), p. 1.

14. *The Death of Ivan Ilych* (New York: Signet, 1960), p. 132.

15. *The Denial of Death* (New York: Macmillan, 1973), p. ix.

16. *On the Overcoming of Fear*, as quoted by J. Pieper, *Death and Immortality* (London: Burns & Oates, 1969), p. 29.

17. *Pensées*, trans. M. Turnell (London: Harper & Row, 1962), p. 174.

18. See J. Choron, *Death and Western Thought* (New York: Collier Books, 1963), pp. 240–54.

19. *Being and Nothingness* (New York: Philosophy Library, 1956), pp. 537, 539.

20. de Tocqueville, *Democracy in America*, op. cit., II, pp. 228–9.

21. See excellent overview by B. Martin, *A Sociology of Contemporary Cultural Change* (Oxford: Basil Blackwell, 1981), p. 1 and *passim*; R. Hewison, *Too Much: Art and Society in the Sixties 1960–75* (London: Methuen, 1986), *passim*; C. Booker, *The Neophiliacs: A Study of the Revolution in English Life in the Fifties and Sixties* (London: Fontana, 1970), *passim*.

22. See H. Marcuse,'The ideology of death' in H. Feifel (ed.), *The Meaning of Death* (New York: McGraw-Hill, 1959), pp. 64–76; *One Dimensional Man* (London: Routledge & Kegan Paul, 1964); and *Eros and Civilisation* (London: Sphere Books, 1969), *passim*.

23. For a critique of Marcuse, see G. Friedman, *The Political Question of the Frankfurt School* (London: Cornell University Press, 1982), pp. 281–87; A. MacIntyre, *Marcuse* (London: Fontana, 1970), *passim*.

24. See C. Lasch, *The Culture of Narcissism: American Life in an Age of Diminishing Expectations* (New York: Warner, 1979), p. 354 and *passim*.

25. See 'The pornography of death', *Encounter*, no. 5 (October 1955), pp. 49–52, and *Death, Grief and Mourning* (London: Cresset Press, 1965), p. 42.

26. 'Current problems in Christology' in *Theological Investigations*, I (Baltimore: Helicon; London: Darton, Longman & Todd, 1961), p. 165; see also W. B. Frazier, 'Death and incarnation' in W. B. Frazier *et al.* (eds), *Death and Ministry* (New York: Seabury, 1975), pp. 262–75.

27. See E. Waugh, *The Loved One: An Anglo-American Tragedy* (Bristol: Chapman & Hall, n.d.), *passim*.

28. E. Waugh, 'Death in Hollywood', *Life* (4 September 1947), pp. 74, 83.

29. Waugh, *The Loved One*, op. cit., pp. 21f.

30. Ibid., p. 128.
31. Cited by C. W. Lane, *Evelyn Waugh* (Boston: Twayne, 1981), p. 105.
32. *The American Way of Death* (New York: Simon & Schuster, 1963), p. 15.
33. *Inventing the American Way of Death, 1820–1920* (Philadelphia: Temple University Press, 1980), p. 221.
34. *Death: The Final Stage of Growth* (Englewood Cliffs, NJ: Prentice-Hall, 1975), p. xxii.
35. *On Death and Dying* (New York: Macmillan, 1969), *passim*.
36. Farrell, *Inventing the American Way of Death*, op. cit., pp. 223f.
37. J. Pieper, *Death and Immortality* (London: Burns & Oates, 1969), pp. 30f.

PART TWO

The Grieving Process in the Scriptures

O brothers, let us leave the shame and sin
  Of taking vainly, in a plaintive mood,
  The holy name of *Grief!*—holy herein,
That by the grief of One came all our good
  (E. B. Browning, *Sonnets: Exaggeration*).

Chapter 4

'CALL THE MOURNING WOMEN . . .':
LOSS AND NEWNESS IN THE
OLD TESTAMENT

We are all mortal; we are like water spilt on the ground, which cannot be gathered up again . . . (2 Sam 14:14).

For look, I am going to create new heavens and a new earth, and the past will not be remembered and will come no more to mind. . . . No more will the sound of weeping be heard there . . . (Is 65:17, 19).

Almost every chapter and page in the Old Testament refers to death, its symptoms, and causes: either the death of a person, or metaphorical death, such as personal and national alienation from Yahweh through sin, sickness, plagues, famine, wars, exile. Indeed, misery, death, and chaos are never at rest in the Old Testament.

However, from time to time, in vivid opposition to this frequent experience of personal and corporate distress and grief, there are eruptions of surprising, even dramatic, newness. Take, for example, that most poignant poetic expression of grief, David's lament over Saul and Jonathan: 'By your dying I too am stricken, I am desolate for you' (2 Sam 1:25). Then David in the depth of his mourning consults Yahweh, and the latter calls David to a startlingly new leadership role: 'Go up! . . . To Hebron. . . . The men of Judah came, and there they anointed David as king of the House of Judah' (2 Sam 2:1, 4).

In this chapter we will look more closely at this loss–grief/ newness paradigm within the Old Testament. The paradigm is sharply evident, not only in the traditional Israelite mourning rituals, but especially within the psalms (and the Lamentations)—the prayerful recording of Israel's encounter over a very long period with the God of Surprises, with other nations, and herself. These religious words became an integral part of community worship and they tell us much about the way in which the Israelites were *expected* to react to significant loss in their lives.

Reflections on death and mourning rituals

Death is a fact of life to the Israelites, the normal consequence of being a creature of God. 'Yahweh gave', Job prays, 'Yahweh has taken back. Blessed be the name of Yahweh!' (1:21). There is no attempt to deny the inevitablity and total finality of death; God alone is immortal (Ps 90:1–6).

The insight that death is related to sin is to be found in Genesis 2:17 and Wisdom 1:12ff., but this point remains somewhat underdeveloped throughout the Old Testament. After death the deceased continued to exist in some temporary, non-dynamic, or passive form in Sheol, though from time to time there are some very faint expressions of hope that death is not the end of life (see Ps 73:23ff.). What is of crucial importance to the Israelite is this: the deceased is only a human being whose life has value not in terms of any after-life, but simply in terms of the *way* it has been lived. The wise Israelite would ponder the inevitability of death, not as a reminder to prepare for the after-life, but as an incentive to live life according to the covenant requirements of Yahweh: 'Teach us to count up the days that are ours, and we shall come to the heart of wisdom' (Ps 90:12).

A death was thought to be good, if certain conditions had been fulfilled: the normal life span must have been achieved—120 years according to Genesis 6:3, 70 years, according to Psalm 90:10; there must be many children to carry on one's name; and evidence that one has lived in the service of Yahweh. There is reason to grieve without restraint if sickness, disaster, or sinful action threatens to cut short an individual's or the nation's life. The person or nation can do nothing from the grave: 'As for a human person—his days are like grass, he blooms like the wild flowers; as soon as the wind blows he is gone, never to be seen there again' (Ps 103:15f.).

The fear of losing through death contact with Yahweh's believing and worshipping community becomes increasingly evident, as Walther Eichrodt notes, as Israelites become more knowledgeable about what is meant by the covenant community. The loss of one's links with the community destroys one's identity and union with Yahweh.[1] If premature death is likely, then the true Israelite would remind the Lord that the dead can no longer be present with the living to worship him: 'Do you work wonders for the dead, can shadows rise up to praise you? Do they speak in the grave of your faithful love, of your constancy in the place of perdition? . . . You have deprived me of friends and companions, and all that I know is the dark' (Ps 88:10f., 18).

There were definite mourning rituals on the death of a relative or in times of national crisis.[2] Mourners tore their clothes and dressed in sackcloth. We read that 'David then took hold of his clothes and tore them, and all the men with him did the same. They mourned and wept and fasted until the evening for Saul and his son Jonathan' (2 Sam 1:11f.). Following his defeat at Ai, a national disaster, Joshua 'tore his clothes and . . . the elders of Israel did the same, and all poured dust on their heads' (Josh 7:6).

Many mourning rites resemble those still widely found in traditional cultures, such as described in Chapter 2 above, having precisely the same overall articulating/legitimizing and prescriptive functions for the individuals and the communities involved. There is a definite order to the rites as the prophet Zechariah points out (12:11–14); for example, tears were to be shed but only at the appropriate time (Mal 2:13). Professional mourners (Am 5:16f.; Eccl 12:5), and particularly women (Jer 9:16, 19; 49:3), were to be intimately involved in the ritual to remind people that death has occurred and grief must be openly expressed. Jeremiah records with pathos the desperate need for mourning women to rally the nation to grieve, because it has lost its roots through exile:

> Prepare to call for the mourning women!
> Send for those who are best at it!
> Let them lose no time in raising the lament over us!
> Let our eyes rain tears,
> our eyelids run with weeping! . . .
> For we must leave the country,
> our homes have been knocked down! (9:16–18).

During the mourning period for the deceased, friends would bring food for the relatives of the deceased (Jer 16:7; Ez 24:17, 22) and they would sit with them to express solidarity or support (Job 2:12f.).

Formal mourning could continue for seven days (Gen 50:10), thirty days (Dt 34:8), or even longer. However, the ending of the liminal period of mourning would be clearly marked;[3] thus, we are told that the mourning time for Moses is concluded:

'The days of weeping for the mourning rites of Moses came to an end' (Dt 34:8). It was expected that people should now be ready to return to active life and to a readjusted set of relationships. Grief must be expressed, but the common good demanded that it did not become chronic, otherwise peace and good order would break down. Thus, David's mourning for his son Absalom had become too protracted and it threatened to undermine his military leadership and the welfare of his soldiers. He had to be told bluntly by his friend Joab that the time for mourning was over and the future had to be faced constructively:

> Today you have made all your servants feel ashamed—today, when they have saved your life . . . because you love those who hate you and hate those who love you. . . . Now get up, come out and reassure your soldiers; for if you do not come out, I swear . . . not one man will stay with you tonight (2 Sam 19:6, 8).

David was brought back to reality and speedily did what he was told, apparently with a renewed self-confidence: 'The king got up and took his seat at the gate. . . . So the king started home and reached the Jordan' (2 Sam 19:9, 16). The paradigm—mourning–desolation/newness—is again demonstrated.

Psalms and laments: newness out of chaos

The psalms are a collection of prayers, used at different times and on various occasions by the Israelties to convey thanksgiving, joy, sorrow, despair, and urgent needs. They depict the whole range of human experience and of the religious life of Israel—grounded in a particular period of history and yet timeless in their meaning and expression. Because these religious lyrics embrace so many human emotions, most quite logically became integral to Israelite (and later Christian) liturgical worship.

About one-third of the psalms are prayers of lament, that is, the speaker grieves or laments over losses or misfortunes—for example, community or personal disasters like plagues, the fear of sudden death or national destruction—and begs Yahweh for help and deliverance. Our immediate concern in this chapter are these community and individual lament psalms.[4]

The two functions of ritual are sharply evident in these lament psalms. Thus they articulate and legitimize the grief feelings of the community or individual. Listen to this opening verse of Psalm 137 in which the exiled Israelite community mourns with deep pathos its exile in Babylon. As in every lament psalm, there is a dramatic recognition of loss:

> By the rivers of Babylon
> we sat and wept
> at the memory of Zion.

The people feel deep in their hearts the loneliness and oppression that comes from being in a foreign and hostile land. The psalm allows them to articulate this pain over and over again, reassuring them that it is quite fitting to do so. However, the ritual structure or form of the lament psalm also prescribes the way in which people must mourn to achieve a new relationship with Yahweh. Walter Brueggemann makes the same points, though in a slightly different way. The form of a lament psalm

> enhances experience and brings it to articulation and also limits the experience of suffering so that it can be received and coped with according to the perspectives, perceptions, and resources of the community. . . . By the use of the form the grief experience is made bearable and, it is hoped, meaningful.[5]

In this highly stimulating article on the form (or ritual) nature of the lament psalms, Brueggemann sees that Elisabeth Kübler-Ross's insight into the grieving process (namely, the denial–isolation, anger, bargaining, depression, and acceptance phases) is an effort to structure a ritual for people in a contemporary world that has lost the art of relating constructively to significant loss.[6] This ritual process of Kübler-Ross contains the two key functions of all rituals: it *articulates/legitimizes* what people may commonly experience in loss; it also *prescribes* how they should act in expressing their emotions in grief situations.

Table 4.1 contrasts the stages of the grief process of the lament psalms with that described by Kübler-Ross. Brueggemann recognizes that there are some similarities in the two ritual processes. For example, both assume that those who grieve move from an experience of chaos or turmoil to an inner peace, requiring a trusted person or group to accompany them on their journey.

Table 4.1

Kübler-Ross[7]	Lament psalm[8]
Denial and isolation	Address to God
Anger	Complaint (e.g. anger)
Bargaining	Expression of trust
Depression	Petition
Acceptance	Assurance
	Vow to praise

Anger, the second stage of Kübler-Ross's model, has its counterpart in the lament psalm. In the former model the sufferers may lash out at loyal relatives or friends, even blaming them for the misery they experience. The latter, however, because they belong to a culture that encourages the denial of loss, rarely know how to cope with such anger; they themselves become annoyed and frustrated at what they see as serious ingratitude on the part of those experiencing misfortune.

The pattern, however, in the lament psalms is significantly different. Here, anger is recognized as a powerful human expression that must not be suppressed. Because the people are united in one covenant with Yahweh, they have every right to let their partner know what they feel about their sufferings and how he is involved in helping to cause them. They know he can 'handle it'. Thus in Psalm 80, we read:

> You have made tears their food . . .
> You let our neighbours quarrel over us,
> our enemies mock us (vv. 5f.).

The people want to make their problems Yahweh's problems. Then, it is hoped, Yahweh will be obligated to do something refreshing about them.[9]

There are several highly notable differences between the two ritual processes. In particular, in contrast to the Kübler-Ross stage of denial and feeling of isolation, a lament psalm starkly proclaims from the beginning that the psalmist or the community is afflicted. There is no camouflaging of the loss. So miserable is the sufferer that there is nothing left but to trust Yahweh. The declaration of trust sparks off a hope-filled petition to Yahweh at the stage when in Kübler-Ross's framework there is a bargaining that leads to depression. In the grief psalms, no matter how horrible the situation may be, there is still the hope that Yahweh will intervene, just as he has repeatedly done in the past. Listen to the psalmist as he ponders the desperate situation confronting the Israelites after the capture of Jerusalem by the Babylonians:

> Shepherd of Israel, listen . . .
> bring us back,
> let your face shine on us and we shall be safe . . .
> . . . . protect what your own hand has planted.
> They have thrown it on the fire like dung,
> the frown of your rebuke will destroy them (Ps 80:1, 7, 15f.).

The psalmist retells the actions of Yahweh that have molded the Israelites into his chosen people: the exodus from Egypt and the entrance into the promised land (vv. 8–11). These interventions of God gave meaning to their lives then; the hope is that he will again intervene to restore meaning in the midst of their fearful misery and chaos (vv. 16f.). The lament proceeds from petition to trust and praise: 'give us life and we will call upon your name' (v. 18).

The words of assurance in the lament psalms and the stage of acceptance in Kübler-Ross's model at first sight may appear to have an identical function. For her, 'acceptance' seems to mean the same thing as a stoic resignation in the face of the inevitable. But this view is contrary to a fundamental assumption in the lament psalms, for there, while death is known to be inevitable, there is always the historically supported belief that Yahweh can transform every crisis into a stunning *new* beginning. The task of covenant members is never to give up hope. That is the mark of every true Israelite.[10]

Brueggemann does not denigrate the importance of Kübler-Ross's model (or other stage theories of grieving) as an aid to understanding what may happen when people are confronted with the basic fear of chaos, death, or significant loss. Rather, his aim is to show that those with faith similar to that of Old Testament believers see things at a quite different level. They do not deny the reality of loss. On the contrary, they see chaos as the occasion to rediscover the historical fact that the Lord can intervene in human affairs to 'create new heavens and a new earth . . . [where] no more will the sound of weeping be heard' (Is 65:17, 19).

The psalms in the social drama of life

In a second stimulating article, Brueggemann[11] uses an insight of Paul Ricoeur to highlight the relevance of the psalms for all stages of the community's and the individual's life cycle or life journey.[12] Ricoeur repeats a basic anthropological fact of life: we yearn for a sense of identity and belonging and we dread chaos, its enemy. Once we have this gift of identity (at what is termed the *orientation stage*), we do everything we can to avoid losing it; if we do lose this identity, we often deny that it has been destroyed.

Ricoeur claims that individuals and groups experience within themselves two identifiable movements that are in dialectical tension: on the one hand, the movement to cling to what has been lost as a source of a much needed sense of belonging and, on the other hand, the ability to go out and grasp a revitalized identity in a new world. It is in times of crisis or chaos, personal/cultural *disorientation* or dislocation, that these two movements are especially in tension. The urge to hold on to the old or to dream of nostalgically returning to the past to rest there, Ricoeur says, is generally more powerful than the desire to move forward to embrace the new. However, the countermovement of reorientation occurs when this pull to escape into the past is overcome and people experience the surprise of a new reality. Though links with the past remain, the emphasis, however, is on *newness*.[13] The three stages of Ricoeur (orientation/disorientation/reorientation) resemble in many significant ways the stages of the ritual process of Victor Turner as explained in Chapter 2: societas (orientation)/liminality (disorientation)/reorientation (reaggregation).

Brueggemann believes that many of the psalms reflect the experiences of the three stages as set out by Ricoeur; thus, he says, there are psalms of orientation, disorientation and reorientation. And because of the similarities between the stages of Ricoeur and those of Turner, we can also speak of psalms of peace/order (societas), chaos (liminality), and newness (reaggregation). I believe that the insights of Brueggemann, Ricoeur, and Turner, when combined, deeply enrich our understanding of the spirituality of grieving (see Figure 4.1).

1. The psalms of *orientation* (e.g. 1, 104, 145) express joy, gratitude to God for his creation and many blessings, and

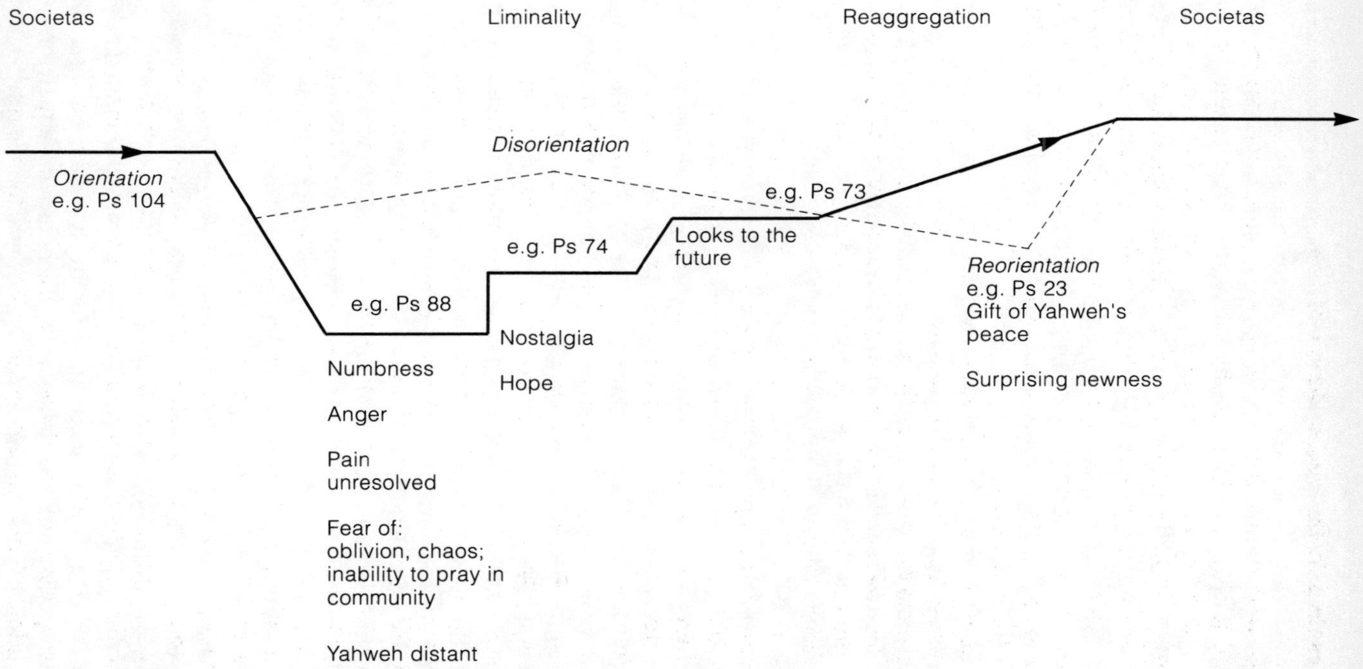

Figure 4.1 Journeying with Yahweh

praise of the covenant. The world is pictured as an *orderly* place without tension or conflict; for example, Psalm 37 provides people with wise, practical guidelines for maintaining harmony in the world. Hence, we read:

> Refrain from anger, leave rage aside,
> do not get heated—it can do no good;
> for evil-doers will be annihilated,
> while those who hope in Yahweh shall have the land
> for their own (vv. 8f.).

The writer of Psalm 104 praises the magnificence and order/balance of Yahweh's creation:

> Yahweh, my God, how great you are! . . .
> You fixed the earth on its foundations . . .
> How countless are your works, Yahweh,
> all of them made so wisely!
> The earth is full of your creatures . . .
> They all depend upon you,
> to feed them when they need it (vv. 1, 5, 24, 27).

2. The psalms of *disorientation* or *dislocation* are the lament psalms. The writers speak of the chaos (for example, sickness, alienation from Yahweh or friends, exile) gravely affecting their lives as individuals or as the nation Israel. The former sense of order and serenity is shattered and this is articulated in powerfully emotive expressions: anger, self-pity, the sense of utter loneliness, hatred.

As mentioned earlier, several years ago I became gravely ill. Up to this point in my life I had maintained over many years a constant and orderly pattern of research, writing and travel in robust good health. One afternoon the surgeon entered my room and without any preliminary comments said: 'I think you have cancer and I think it is very serious.' With that he left the room. I felt numb. The surgeon could not have been speaking about me! I turned to the Book of Psalms and accidentally I chanced on Psalm 88 with its subtitle: 'Prayer for one who is gravely ill'. As I read the psalm it was as though I had written it myself, for every word expressed my feelings of shattering desolation and helplessness. I simply could not believe that I had ever seen the psalm before, though I had in fact recited it at least monthly for thirty years! Let us look closely at this remarkable psalm, which has no equal for its expression of almost unrelieved chaos and loneliness.[14]

The psalm has several desperation-filled petitions for help from Yahweh—for example, 'I cry out to you in the night' (v. 1), 'I cry to you, Yahweh, every morning my prayer comes before you' (v. 13). Yet Yahweh does not answer. There is simply no response. Yahweh is there, for the psalmist has a deep and abiding faith, but Yahweh will give no sign whatso-ever that he is listening, or even concerned, at the complete breakdown of the psalmist's life of peace and order.

Yahweh's failure to respond, however, does not deter the psalmist, because he only intensifies the anguish of his words: he is being consigned to 'the brink of Sheol' (v. 3), 'left alone among the dead' (v. 5), 'plunged . . . to the bottom of the grave, in the darkness, in the depths' (v. 6). If he is left like this, deprived of all contact with the community of worship, then how can he praise Yahweh?

The psalmist's sense of loneliness is desperate:

> You have deprived me of my friends,
> made me repulsive to them,
> imprisoned, with no escape (v. 8).

Like the psalmist, I could not share my sense of inner loneli-ness with any other person. Once I was strong and in total command of my life, then suddenly I am powerless, com-pletely unable to do anything for myself. My friends would visit me, but often there was an embarrassed conversation about anything but the disease I was suspected of having. A wall of silence had developed between my friends and myself about what really bothered me in the very depth of my being— was I to die? In my hour of need for understanding and consolation, my friends often embarrassingly confined conver-sation to matters of peripheral importance to me—the weather, sport, the latest community happening: 'You have deprived me of friends and companions' (v. 18); 'Already [I am] num-bered among those who sink into oblivion, I am as one bereft of strength' (v. 4). Could I ever again become a dynamic member of community life—giving and not just receiving from the kindnesses of others?

There is unrestrained anger in the psalmist's heart. And it is directed straight at Yahweh, the presumed cause of the psalmist's misery: 'You have plunged me to the bottom of the grave . . . weighted down by your anger, kept low by your waves. You have deprived me of my friends. . . . Your anger has overwhelmed me, your terrors annihilated me' (vv. 6–8, 16). Yahweh is prepared to leave the psalmist in this darkness with no consolation whatsoever: 'I am finished! . . . all that I know is the dark' (vv. 15, 18). Yet, though the psalmist is on the brink of total despair, one senses in the psalmist's voice a simple, unarticulated and unshakeable trust in Yahweh. Without this trust the psalmist would not even be praying.

At the time I 'discovered' this psalm, I was at the lowest point of my personal journey thus far. God did answer my prayer. Deprived of human consolation, I had no alternative but to trust a God who seemed so distant and uncaring; later he responded to that trust with an energizing power of love and compassion. Every time I ponder this experience of personal chaos, he again helps me to see that my life must be directed according to a set of God-centered priorities: 'If Yahweh does not build a house, in vain do its builders toil' (Ps 127:1). Out of my personal chaos there came life beyond all human measure.

Psalm 74 is especially relevant to the theme of this book. The pivotal symbol of Yahweh's presence to the people, the temple, has been destroyed and Yahweh gets all the blame! With the devastation of the temple, the identity of the Israelites as a people is shattered:

God, why have you finally rejected us,
your anger blazing against the flock you used to pasture? . . .
The enemy has sacked everything in the sanctuary . . .
they set fire to your sanctuary,
profanely rased to the ground the dwelling-place of
your name . . . (vv. 1, 3, 7).

And there is no indication that the situation will change: 'We see no signs, no prophet any more, and none of us knows how long it will last' (v. 9). Desolation reigns supreme.

Unlike the composer of Psalm 88, the writer of this psalm looks back to the moment of creation when Yahweh molded the world into an orderly shape out of the primeval chaos:[15] 'You . . . turned primordial rivers into dry land . . . you caused sun and light to exist, you fixed all the boundaries of the earth, you created summer and winter' (vv. 15–17). When the chosen people are threatened in the exodus with destruction from the pursuing Egyptians, Yahweh by his power 'split the sea in two' (v. 13). Now with the temple's destruction new chaos

erupts. Yet Israel, encouraged by such previous dramatic interventions, hopefully anticipates Yahweh will restore order and
identity to the nation: 'Arise, God, champion your own cause'
(v. 22).

Today many religious may identify with the sentiments of
this psalm. With few or no new recruits and with financial
income down, their congregations cannot maintain the large
houses—for example, schools and seminaries—that once symbolized successful apostolates. 'What is our future?' they say,
so in their hearts they cry out: 'We see no signs . . . any more,
and none of us knows how long it will last. . . . Why hold
back your hand, keep your right hand hidden in the folds of
your robe?' (Ps 74:9, 11).

Perhaps some members of religious congregations have
acquired their identity as religious primarily from belonging to
this or that particular apostolate or house. They are in difficulties when their congregation withdraws or closes the latter,
because then they find themselves in a chaos situation, akin
to the experience of the psalmist bemoaning the loss of the
temple. God is rejecting them! Religious, like the psalmist
before them, can and must grieve over the loss of the symbols
of an apparently successful former age. But they must confi-
dently beg the Lord to help them to become detached from
these symbols; then, removed from the haunting power of the
past, they will have the energy to find new ways to witness
to his saving power: 'Do not let the downtrodden retreat in
confusion, give the poor and needy cause to praise your name'
(v. 21). Let them remember the fact that 'God, my king from
the first' (v. 12) will act as he has done in the past to bring
order out of the chaos.

Psalm 73 links a vivid experience of disorientation with a
glimpse of the radical newness of the reorientation stage.[16] The
psalmist is deeply disturbed and puzzled, for he sees the
wicked prosper: 'untroubled, . . . [they are] exempt from
the cares which are the human lot. . . . Cynically they advocate
evil, loftily they advocate force' (vv. 4, 5, 8). He is tempted to
follow their lead: 'My feet were on the point of stumbling. . . .
Was it useless . . . to have kept my own heart clean' (vv. 2,
13). Then he pauses. He asks himself the question: Is there
another way of looking at life, the way of Yahweh? He concludes that ultimately in Yahweh's good time evil will meet its
own destruction:

> You place them on a slippery slope
> and drive them into chaos.
> How sudden their hideous destruction! (vv. 18f.).

This insight is Yahweh's gift, for he could not, he believes, have come to this conclusion by himself, because his own heart had been tempted by the apparent triumphs of the rich and powerful. Only Yahweh could have been the source of a radically new way of looking at the world around him:

> My heart grew embittered,
> my affections dried up,
> I was stupid . . .
> Even so, I stayed in your presence,
> you grasped me by the right hand;
> you will guide me with advice . . . (vv. 21–23).

Those who love and serve Yahweh will be rewarded, those who cynically ignore him will be condemned: 'Indeed God is good to Israel, the Lord to those who are pure of heart. . . . I have made the Lord Yahweh my refuge, to tell of all your works' (vv. 1, 28).

We who struggle to be devout Christians are confronted with a depressing situation, because as believers and churches we just seem to be losing out at every turn. The message of Christ seems more and more irrelevant in the consumer-oriented, highly competitive and capitalistic world. Many fellow Christians have become 'annual' worshippers, or merely content to be married and buried in the local parish church. Yet they seem happy in their love of material things and their refusal to be concerned with the poor. Like the psalmist, we are tempted, when confronted by the departure of parishioners and the closure of non-viable parishes, to join them in their pursuit of 'untroubled . . . comfortable portliness' (v. 4). If we do not give way to this temptation, it is because of God's grace; through this gift we see the world around us with the refreshing eyes of Christ himself: 'Who else is there for me in heaven? And, with you, I lack nothing on earth' (v. 26). This is the hope that energizes the humble, trusting servant of Yahweh.

3. The *reorientation* psalms attest that Yahweh has unexpectedly bestowed new gifts on individuals and on the nation. Just when the psalmists or Israel in the midst of chaos and con-

fusion had almost given up hope of Yahweh intervening, they are suddenly, through Yahweh's generous initiative, showered with *new* gifts. There is now an exciting new creation, a new world of peace, unimagined energy to act in the service of Yahweh. As Brueggemann says, 'The extremity of reorientation is as shattering as that of disorientation'.[17] There must be a celebration to thank and praise Yahweh, and this is precisely the function of the reorientation psalms.

In Psalm 29 we have a superb description of the transcendent power of God. The world is threatened with chaos, but it is no match for Yahweh for nothing can resist his power, even the mighty cedars break under the force of his voice (v. 5). The mighty power of God demands celebration in song and this psalm does this poetically and precisely. Whoever recites or sings this psalm is bound to feel the confidence that God's re-creative power gives to those who love him:

> Yahweh is enthroned as king for ever.
> Yahweh will give strength to his people,
> Yahweh blesses his people with peace (v. 10f.).

We Christians, as we look at the fading influence of our churches, missionary societies, and religious congregations, may, in the depths of our despondency, lose confidence in the power of God in Christ to renew/recreate all things. We need to be repeatedly reminded that the Lord loves us beyond our most extravagant dreams and that 'he makes Lebanon skip like a calf, Sirion like a young wild ox' (v. 6). Out of chaos there will be a newness, but it is a newness that is a gift of the Lord. Our task is to beg for this gift, with every fibre of our being:

> To you Yahweh, I cry,
>   my rock, do not be deaf to me!
> If you stay silent
>   I shall be like those who sink into oblivion (Ps 28:1).

Unquestioned confidence in Yahweh's personal protection, no matter how much suffering the psalmist or Israel has endured, is the theme of Psalm 23. This trust in Yahweh evokes a startlingly novel way of looking at the world; the numbness and loneliness so evident in the dislocation Psalm 88 are put aside, because Yahweh offers his protective presence:

> Yahweh is my shepherd, I lack nothing . . .
> Even were I to walk in a ravine as dark as death
> I should fear no danger, for you are at my side . . . (vv. 1, 4).

Yahweh is here being praised, Artur Weiser tells us, not so much for his presence in the temple, but for his intimate friendship with the psalmist.[18] The Christian who must move from the parish church he or she has come to love over many years, or the religious who must face the loss of a particularly historic house or apostolate to which he or she has become deeply attached, the evangelizer who must put aside irrelevant apostolic methods and risk new approaches, will find this psalm to be challenging and inspiring. They must become through divine benevolence a little more detached, deriving their identity from their union in faith with the Lord and not from this or that fragile human symbol. Let them praise the Lord who resides deep within their hearts—the true houses of the Lord. This undeserved largess of the Lord *is* something to celebrate.

Newness in the Book of Job

The Book of Job is about the sufferings of innocent people.[19] Many Israelites believe that Yahweh rewards the righteous with material well-being, but this contradicts the experience of many God-fearing people. The author of Job in one of the world's finest pieces of literature examines the problem presented in story form and in a series of poems, and he ventures some new solutions to the puzzling issue.

In the opening chapters (1 – 2), Job is the model of the righteous man; he is blessed with many children, good health, social respectability, and large flocks and herds. He has shown justice and compassion to widows, orphans and strangers. For him everything is flourishing. This is the *orientation* stage as illustrated above.

Suddenly, from the beginning of chapter 3, Job's secure world disintegrates because he loses everything: wealth, health, and family. His whole herd is stolen, his children are killed when a house crashes down on them, and he himself is covered in bleeding sores. No one will approach him for fear of getting the same disease, so he sits near the town rubbish dump, pitifully scratching his sores with some broken pottery. Job experiences the misery and loneliness of the *dislocation* stage:

> My days are over, so are my plans, my heart-strings are broken (17:11).

> I have months of futility assigned to me, nights of suffering to be my lot (7:3).

Puzzled, he says to Yahweh: 'Suppose I have sinned, what have I done to you, you tireless watcher of humanity?' (7:20). He gazes nostalgically back to his years of prosperity—the orientation stage. His wife encourages him to curse God and his friends berate him and accuse him of insulting God, but Job continues to call on Yahweh who now seems so utterly inaccessible and seemingly uninterested in his plight: 'Will no one help me to know how to travel to his dwelling?' (23:3). Yet, in the midst of his darkness, Job still has energizing hope: 'I know that I have a living Defender . . . He whom I shall see will take my part' (19:25, 27).

Now comes the *reorientation* experience in which Yahweh responds to Job's bewilderment about the mystery of evil. The world, Job discovers, is alive with the mystery of God's wisdom. In spite of what Job or others might think, God is in charge and he holds all creation together. There is to be no return to primeval chaos. Job is reassured that Yahweh cares for him far more than all the animals; his sufferings have befallen him in line with Yahweh's wisdom, the same wisdom that allows Job to have good health and material prosperity. This insight is *the* discovery for Job, Yahweh's benefaction, so Job ends with a moving prayer of humility, joy, and thanks:

I know that you are all-powerful . . .
Before, I knew you only by hearsay
but now, having seen you with my own eyes,
I retract what I have said, and repent in dust and ashes (42:2, 5f.).

A parish in a poor area is being closed, because ministers cannot be found to staff it, yet there seems to be no shortage of ministers for a wealthy suburb. How, ask the abandoned parishioners, can this be allowed? How can God allow this kind of injustice to happen? One religious congregation is not receiving any vocations at all despite vigorous efforts to attract candidates, but a neighboring congregation is recruiting significant numbers. Where is the Lord in this suffering and loss of congregational strength?

The lesson that Job learnt remains universally relevant. Like Job, we are called to surrender our entire selves to God's all-embracing wisdom and love; hopefully he will give us the same surprising gift of new insight and consolation: 'You have told me about great works that I cannot understand, about marvels which are beyond me, of which I know nothing' (42:3).

Jeremiah: prophet of grief and newness

Jeremiah stands out in the Old Testament as a lonely, tragic person, but he has the skill of using ritual grieving as a way of confronting the Israelites with their sinful ways. They must return to their covenant obligations or face the death of their culture and nation.

Jeremiah grieves over losses at three levels. He sorrows at the sight of his own inadequacies before God and his fellow Israelites; he grieves for and with his people because of their sinfulness before God; Yahweh and he jointly grieve over the calamities that are to befall or have befallen the chosen people because of their arrogant stubbornness. He hopes that through the public sharing of grief at the approaching destruction of the pivotal symbols of Israel's identity—the temple, the city and kingship—the people will acknowledge death and be open to the new promised by Yahweh.[20]

Ponder a little one of the prophet's own personal laments or 'confessions' first (15:10–21). He gives vent to his anguish, describing the abuse he suffers because of his role as a prophet, condemning his enemies and calling for his own vindication. Nothing timid here: 'Have I not genuinely done my best to serve you, Yahweh? . . . avenge me on my persecutors' (15:11, 15). He aggressively reprimands Yahweh for having deceived and deserted him in times of personal abuse at the hands of the mobs, for he has been flung into prison, beaten, shackled, and even lowered down a well: 'Truly, for me you are a deceptive stream with uncertain waters!' (15:18). When he sorrows over his failures as a prophet of Yahweh and his lack of gratitude to a loving companion, Yahweh immediately accepts his repentance—in fact, even before it is requested. Then Jeremiah once more feels the energizing or revitalizing embrace of the Lord in his prophetic task:

> If you repent, I shall restore you to plead before me . . . (15:19).
>
> But Yahweh is at my side like a mighty hero; my opponents will stumble, vanquished, confounded by their failure . . . (20:11).

The tender-minded young man becomes strong and courageous; the sensitive, hesitant prophet becomes 'a pillar of iron, a wall of bronze to stand against the whole country' (1:18). This is the newness, the transformation, the miracle, born out of Jeremiah's repeated proclamation of his grief or failure of nerve.[21]

In this modern age, in which death is denied, the task of confronting people with their denial of personal and structural sins is a most unpopular apostolate, just as it was in the days of Jeremiah. By structural sin we mean those economic, social, or political institutions or ideologies that oppress people and deny them their human rights. Structural sins coalesce to form a culture of oppression, the result ultimately of many concrete acts of power/wealth-hungry individuals. At the time of Jeremiah the rich and politically powerful built a culture of oppression to enslave the poor. It is the same today as millions are humanly crushed by structures that prevent them from being the masters of their own destiny. So we readily identify with Jeremiah as he cringes in fear at the very thought of such a burdensome challenge. Like him, we want to run away, to be spared the sniggers of those who think our evangelical and prophetic role is worthless, bothersome, a relic of a bygone age. In the depths of our hearts, however, we yearn for that Jeremiah-like openness with God, his repentance, his ongoing struggle to die to his false attachments in order to proclaim joyfully: 'he has delivered the soul of one in need from the clutches of evil doers' (20:13).

Reflect on the way in which Yahweh and Jeremiah grieve together over the destruction of Israel. Jeremiah's duty is to call his people to a profound conversion of heart and action. The Babylonians are God's judgment on a highly unfaithful people. Because there is not the faintest move on the people's part to repent, Yahweh, speaking through Jeremiah, insists their culture is doomed; and this saddens Jeremiah to the depths of his heart: 'The wound of the daughter of my people wounds me too . . . I raise the wail and lament for the mountains' (8:21; 9:9). Yet the people continue to deny they are committing evil; Jeremiah is speaking nonsense. For the Israelites, vice is seen as virtue:

> For, from the least to greatest,
> they are all greedy for gain . . .
> all of them practise fraud.
> Without concern they dress my people's wound,
> saying, 'Peace! Peace!'
> Whereas there is no peace (6:13f.).

Jeremiah sees the coming doom as a consequence of the people's loss of friendship with Yahweh. This causes him painful anticipated grief which he graphically expresses in the lament style: 'In the pit of my stomach how great my agony. . . . Ruin on ruin is the news . . . I looked to the earth—it was a formless waste' (4:19, 23). The reducing of Israel to chaos is inevitable because of their 'great guilt and countless sins . . . [their] pain is incurable' (30:15).

Abraham Heschel movingly speaks of the *divine pathos*, the capacity of God himself to suffer because he has entered through the covenant into a personal relationship with Israel-ites. As they suffer, so he suffers.[22] Through the love-inspired covenant God risks being hurt, if his Israelite partners do not live up to their side of the agreement. And this is precisely what happens. Yahweh is forced to allow their destruction because the people are so sinfully stubborn. Yet, because of Yahweh's intimate union with them he is also attacking himself: 'Yahweh says this: Now I am knocking down what I have built, am uprooting what I have planted, over the whole country!' (45:4). Yahweh is thrown into a state of mourning the loss of his people and even of himself:[23]

> Yahweh Sabaoth says this . . .
> Let them lose no time in raising the lament over us!
> Let our eyes rain tears,
> our eyelids run with weeping! (9:16–17).

Yet, just when all seems to be totally lost, Yahweh in his grief becomes the savior of himself and of the same people he is condemning to devastation. Yahweh's original words to Jere-miah are to be fulfilled: 'Look, today I have set you over the nations and kingdoms, to uproot and to knock down, to destroy and to overthrow, to build and to plant' (1:10). Yahweh, though his heart is torn apart with the sorrow of mourning, reiterates his willingness to build the nation anew, for he can no longer tolerate the people being mocked by other nations for their weaknesses and destruction: 'I shall restore you to health and heal your wounds . . . you who used to be called "Outcast", "Zion for whom no one cares" ' (30:17). Yahweh is depicted as one who is so moved by the intensity of his anguish over the loss of his chosen people, that he can no longer hold back his recreative power.

The lesson is clear: when one wholeheartedly admits that death has occurred, only then will one be disposed to see the need for new life. If the pain is publicly expressed and embraced, as Yahweh himself does when he loses his covenant relationship with Israel, then 'it liberates God to heal'.[24]

God in Christ is a partner in the founding and maintenance of every method or structure of evangelization—for example, a school, a parish, an evangelization program, a religious congregation. When these structures—for whatever reason—lose their dynamism or must cease to exist, then God suffers! There is divine pathos. We owe it to him and to all people past and present who have been involved in the apostolic projects to heed the words of Yahweh: 'Let them lose no time in raising the lament over us!' (9:17). Let the ritual prescribe a mourning that acknowledges not only past and present apostolic successes, but also the opportunities lost to preach the Word of God through sinful or unconscious neglect. Give ample space to mourn, in faith with the Lord, that which is lost, 'For we must leave the country, our homes have been knocked down!' (9:18). Listen to the Lord speaking in our grief; he will call us to a new way of preaching the Good News, if admitting death we are prepared to cry *to* and *with* him:

> Yahweh, for your name's sake, intervene!
> Yes, our acts of infidelity have been many . . .
> Yahweh, hope of Israel,
> its Saviour in time of distress . . .
> We are called by your name.
> Do not desert us! (14:7, 8, 9).

Summary

As Bernhard Anderson observes, the Israelite prophets and the psalmists use the imagery of chaos in order to highlight its opposite; namely, the ongoing inventive and redemptive action of God.[25] The experience of significant loss is likened to chaos: anger, numbness, loss of identity, denial that loss has occurred, nostalgia for the familiar past, guilt over one's failures and sins, depression, fear of the future, a feeling of drifting without purpose and identity, the sense that God has withdrawn his protecting presence. Yet, participation in chaos can be the preface for an experience of God's ever-renewing love, provided we are prepared to grieve over that which has been lost.

The Old Testament is filled with calls to sorrow over what has been destroyed or broken down, if there is to be new life; through the psalms we are even taught *how* to grieve. Particularly in the lament psalms we are constantly reminded that no matter how chaotic our condition may be, God has the power to do the humanly impossible—to lift us out of 'the seething chasm, from the mud of the mire'. He can 'set my feet on rock' and make 'my footsteps firm . . . a fresh song in my mouth' (Ps 40:2, 3).[26] Lament psalms, writes Claus Westermann, transform the experience of liminality chaos into a way of approaching 'God with abandonment that permits daring and visioning and even ecstasy'.[27]

The call to grieve over loss is directed to both the individual Israelite and the corporate person or the nation. Yahweh made a covenant with the people corporately so that when they experience chaos they must grieve as a whole (see Figure 4.2); if they grieve with converting hearts, then, God willing, the nation will relive the re-creating power of the Exodus, the time when God first freely formed them out of nothing.

In the next chapter we see that in Jesus Christ, the Messiah, the Anointed One of the Father, we have the triumph of God's Kingdom over all the powers of evil, darkness, or chaos.[28] If we follow his example of grieving, then we will discover through his love what it means to be in 'the new heavens and new earth' (2 Pet 3:13).

Discussion questions

1. What insight in this chapter most appeals to the group? Why?
2. What does 'liminality chaos' mean when applied to the Old Testament? Can members of the group, or the group itself, identify with

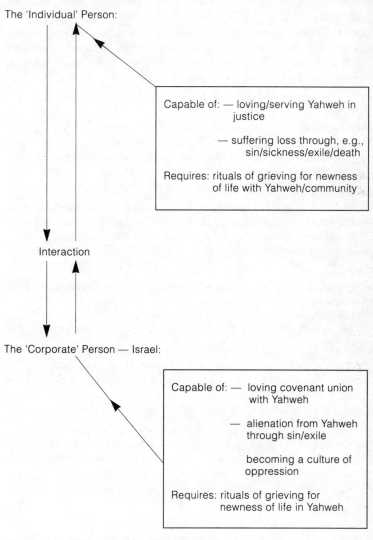

The 'Individual' Person:

Capable of: — loving/serving Yahweh in
justice

— suffering loss through, e.g.,
sin/sickness/exile/death

Requires: rituals of grieving for newness
of life with Yahweh/community

Interaction

The 'Corporate' Person — Israel:

Capable of: — loving covenant union
with Yahweh

— alienation from Yahweh
through sin/exile

becoming a culture of
oppression

Requires: rituals of grieving for
newness of life in Yahweh

Figure 4.2 'Person' in the Old Testament

the meaning of this expression from their own experience? Do they wish to share this with the group?

3. What psalm described in the chapter particularly appeals to the group? Why?

4. Could the group identify some loss that it is experiencing? If so, encourage some individual(s) to work with the group to prepare a ritual of mourning, based on the structure of the lament psalms, in which the group can eventually share.

References

1. *The Theology of the Old Testament* (London: SCM Press, 1967), pp. 497–529.
2. See L. R. Bailey, *Biblical Perspectives on Death* (Philadelphia: Fortress Press, 1979), p. 35; R. de Vaux, *Ancient Israel: Its Life and Institutions* (London: Darton, Longman & Todd, 1961), pp. 56–61.
3. See G. J. Botterweck and H. Ringgren (eds), *Theological Dictionary of the Old Testament* (Grand Rapids: W. B. Eerdmans, 1975), pp. 45f., 118.
4. See C. Westermann, *The Psalms: Structures, Content, and Message* (Minneapolis: Augsburg, 1980), pp. 10–28; J. F. Craghan, *The Psalms: Prayers for the Ups, Downs and In-Betweens of Life* (Wilmington, DE: Michael Glazier, 1985), pp. 115–67.
5. 'The formfulness of grief', *Interpretation: A Journal of Bible and Theology*, vol. 31, no. 3 (1977), p. 265.
6. Ibid., pp. 267–75.
7. See E. Kübler-Ross, *On Death and Dying* (New York: Macmillan, 1969), *passim*.
8. See C. Westermann, *The Praise of God in the Psalms* (London: Epworth Press, 1965), pp. 52–71, and *Praise and Lament in the Psalms* (Atlanta: John Knox, 1981), *passim*; A. Weiser, *The Psalms: A Commentary* (London: SCM Press, 1962), pp. 66–83.
9. See W. Brueggemann, *The Message of the Psalms: A Theological Commentary* (Minneapolis: Augsburg, 1984), p. 54.
10. See Brueggemann, 'The formfulness of grief', op. cit., p. 273.
11. 'Psalms and the life of faith: a suggested typology of function', *The Journal for the Study of the Old Testament*, vol. 17 (1980), pp. 3–32.
12. See 'Biblical hermeneutics', *Semeia*, vol. 4 (1975), pp. 1–21.
13. See comments by P. Ricoeur, *The Conflict of Interpretations: Essays in Hermeneutics* (Evanston: Northwestern University Press, 1974), pp. 369f. and *passim*.
14. See Brueggemann, *The Message of the Psalms*, op. cit., pp. 78–80, and 'A shape for Old Testament theology, II: Embrace of pain', *The Catholic Biblical Quarterly*, vol. 47, no. 3 (1985), pp. 403f.
15. *The Message of the Psalms*, op. cit., p. 70; see also G. Arbuckle, *Out of Chaos: Refounding Religious Congregations* (New York: Paulist Press, 1988), pp. 47–62; and B. W. Anderson, *Creation Versus Chaos: The Reinterpretation of Mythical Symbolism in the Bible* (New York: Association Press, 1967), pp. 132–7 and *passim*.

16. See Craghan, *The Psalms*, op. cit., pp. 185–8; and Brueggemann, *The Message of the Psalms*, op. cit., pp. 115–21.
17. 'Psalms and the life of faith', op. cit., p. 10.
18. Weiser, *The Psalms*, op. cit., p. 231.
19. For commentaries, see J. F. Craghan, *The Psalms*, op. cit., p. 22; J. E. Hartley, *The Book of Job* (Grand Rapids: W. B. Eerdmans, 1988); J. G. Janzen, 'Job' in *Interpretation: A Bible Commentary for Teaching and Preaching* (Atlanta: John Knox Press, 1985); M. H. Pope, *Job* (New York: Doubleday, 1965).
20. See W. Brueggemann, *The Prophetic Imagination* (Philadelphia: Fortress Press, 1978), p. 111, and 'The Book of Jeremiah: portrait of the prophet' in J. L. Mays and P. J. Achtemeier (eds), *Interpreting the Prophets* (Philadelphia: Fortress Press, 1987), pp. 113–29.
21. See J. Bright, 'A prophet's lament and its answer: Jeremiah 15:10–21' in L. G. Perdue and B. W. Kovacs (eds), *A Prophet to the Nations: Essays in Jeremiah Studies* (Winona Lake: Eisenbrauns, 1984), pp. 325–47; G. Von Rad, *The Message of the Prophets* (London: SCM Press, 1968), pp. 161–88.
22. A. Heschel, *The Prophets: An Introduction* (New York: Harper & Row, 1969), p. 24.
23. Ibid., p. 111.
24. W. Brueggemann, *Hopeful Imagination: Prophetic Voices in Exile* (Philadelphia: Fortress Press, 1986), p. 43.
25. *Creation Versus Chaos: The Reinterpretation of Mythical Symbolism in the Bible* (New York: Association Press, 1967), p. 132 and *passim*; also W. Brueggemann, 'Kinship and chaos: a study in tenth century theology', *The Catholic Biblical Quarterly*, vol. 33 (1971), pp. 317–32, and 'Weariness, exile and chaos: A motif in royal theology', *The Catholic Biblical Quarterly*, vol. 34 (1972), pp. 19–38.
26. See B. Anderson, *Out of the Depths: The Psalms Speak for Us Today* (Philadelphia: Westminster Press, 1983), p. 76 and *passim*.
27. *Elements of Old Testament Theology*, trans. D. Scott (Atlanta: John Knox Press, 1982), p. 103.
28. Ibid., p. 162.

Chapter 5

JESUS CALLS: MOURN THAT WE MAY BE RECREATED

Blessed are those who mourn: they shall be comforted (Mt 5:5).

In all truth I tell you, you will be weeping and wailing while the world will rejoice; you will be sorrowful, but your sorrow will turn to joy (Jn 16:20).

Several years ago I witnessed the last faith-filled hours of a young man dying of cancer. As he lapsed into unconsciousness his mother knelt beside him and whispered into his ear a grieving prayer: 'Kevin', she said, 'you are in the Garden with Jesus. Walk with him, let go! Go to the Father. Mary is with you to help you!' What an extraordinary scene! Little could more vividly express the dramatic difference between the Old and the New Testaments than the gentle hope-inspired example of this mother. This chapter is about why this mother could show hope and peace, when confronted with such human loss.

Readers will recall that the ideal death for the Israelites was to be achieved in the fullness of old age with undiminished powers (Gen 25:8). Life ceased at death. Now, however, in the New Testament, death is seen as an effect of primeval disobedience (Rom 5:18f.). If sin can be overcome, then mortality can be effectively prevented through the coming of a new Adam; his death and resurrection mean that death has lost its power (1 Cor 15:45–49). The grieving mother believed this. So did her son. This belief gave them hope that there will be a time in which there will be no more death, and no more mourning.

In the Old Testament several writers rather hesitantly express the hope that there be life after death; in the New Testament this hope that there can be a victory over forces of chaos in all its mortal forms is confirmed and affirmed in the death and rising of Christ. Biological death continues, but its meaning is profoundly changed, for now, after the death of

Jesus, it is not the end of our life, but rather the beginning of our life in an unimagined fullness or newness:

> This perishable nature of ours must put on imperishability, this mortal nature must put on immortality . . . then will the words of scripture come true: *Death is swallowed up in victory. Death, where is your victory? Death, where is your sting?* (1 Cor 15:53–55).

We become one in the death of Christ and one in the hope of his resurrection.

> I am the resurrection.
> Anyone who believes in me, even though that person dies, will live,
> and whoever lives and believes in me will never die (Jn 11:25f.).

Dying/grieving for the kingdom

The mission of Jesus is to proclaim the kingdom of God. In Daniel the kingdom to be established by God will 'shatter and absorb all the previous kingdoms and itself will last for ever' (2:44); John the Baptist preaches that 'the kingdom of Heaven is close at hand' (Mt 3:1). But Jesus does not foretell the coming of the kingdom. Instead, in his ministry he *proclaims* that the kingdom is alive within us (Mt 12:28) and confirms its presence by his actions. He breaks through the symptoms of human death—mortality and sin—by healing the sick, forgiving sins on his own kingly authority, driving out the demons of the kingdom of this world, and by raising the dead.

People must not expect to share in the kingdom automatically; they must work to build it in this world: 'It is not anyone who says to me, "Lord, Lord", who will enter the kingdom of Heaven, but the person who does the will of my Father in heaven' (Mt 7:21). We live in the time of transition, the in-between-time, in which the kingdom of God is present to us through faith; the fullness of the kingdom has yet to come, when 'the first earth' will have 'disappeared' and 'the new Jerusalem [will come] down out of heaven from God, prepared as a bride dressed for her husband' (Rev 21:1f.). These transition times must be marked by repentance and the struggle to work with Christ in justice and love, thus witnessing, even though imperfectly, to the fullness of a 'new heaven and a new earth' yet to come.

This twofold aspect of the kingdom as present and future reality is made plain in the parables of Jesus about the kingdom (Mt 13; 18:23–35; 20:1–16; 25:1–13; Mk 4; Lk 8:4–18; 13:18–21). In the parables, the kingdom already exists, but at the same time it must be nurtured until its fullness in the times of the final harvest under the direction of Jesus the King. Those who are already part of Christ's kingdom in this transition stage through repentance and faith actually begin to live what St Paul calls 'a new life' (Rom 6:4). They enjoy the fruits of the Spirit of the Lord: 'love, joy, peace, patience, kindness, goodness, trustfulness, gentleness and self-control' (Gal 5:22).

Thus, these days are a period of trial for 'we must . . . experience many hardships before we enter' fully into 'the kingdom of God' (Acts 14:22). It is an ongoing battle against the seductive powers of the kingdom of this world, but it is the *hope* of the new heaven and new earth that motivates us to be strong and persistent in this struggle to be Christ to the world. This struggle is described by Christ as a process of daily dying to self, a journey of detaching oneself from all that would keep one from the Lord: 'If anyone wants to be a follower of mine, let him renounce himself and take up his cross and follow me. Anyone who wants to save his life will lose it; but anyone who loses his life for my sake, and for the sake of the gospel, will save it' (Mk 8:34f.). Our priority is kingdom-seeking and the letting go of all that interferes with this priority: 'Set your hearts on his kingdom first, and on God's saving justice, and all these other things will be given you as well' (Mt 6:33).

'Letting go' means mourning

He or she who dies lives a new life! This paradox, namely that blessings are bestowed not because of one's worldly good luck, but because of self-denial or what the world considers folly, is further eloquently summarized in the beatitudes of Jesus.

In the Old Testament beatitudes are declarations frequently to be found in the psalms. They describe the kind of rewards promised for the righteous; for example, earthly benefits like peace, prosperity, plentiful descendants, the joys of temple worship.[1] The beatitudes in the New Testament, as set out by the evangelists Matthew and Luke, are similar in structure to their Old Testament counterparts, but they significantly differ in the kind of reward promised the righteous. The New Testament beatitudes stress the joy of participation in the kingdom of God, especially in its fulfillment at the end of time, rather than rewards in this earthly life.

The third beatitude of Matthew's listing is: 'Blessed are those who mourn: they shall be comforted' (5:5). The mourning (or grieving) here refers to a supernatural sorrow in contrast to worldly sorrow. When we enter into our own inner chaos of personal sinfulness, we discover that we are nothing without the power and loving presence of God in Christ, the one who alone can ultimately hold back the forces of evil or chaos.[2] We recognize that through sin we lose this crucial awareness of how much Jesus loves us, and this causes us intense sorrow or grief (see Figure 5.1).

This all-important self-knowledge is a gift of the Lord, for we cannot confront our own inner chaos and sinfulness without the strength that comes from Christ. It would be so terrifying we would go mad, and this is precisely what St Paul means when he cries out: 'What a wretched man I am! Who will rescue me from this body doomed to death? God—thanks be to him—through Jesus Christ our Lord' (Rom 7:24f.).

The Christian who mourns does not stop at his or her own sinfulness, but grieves also because of the sins of others in one's community, neighborhood, the nation, and the whole world. Sin is seen to be at the root of racism, the oppression and sufferings of the poor, the arrogance of the rich and powerful. The poor, the helpless, and deprived are to be the special concern of those who mourn, because they are often the objects of ruthless oppression of the wealthy: 'be sad with those in sorrow' (Rom 12:15). It was particularly to the powerless that Jesus came (Mt 11:5). So often, because of the sinful structures that oppress them, the powerless come to believe that they are humanly inferior to the powerful. If they can be helped to mourn according to the Gospel image, they will discover the source of their sufferings and the liberating power of Christ's saving grace; from Jesus they will receive the gift of hope that will inspire them to struggle for justice. Oppressors have cause to fear those who mourn in Christ.

Mourning is the duty not just of the individual but of the congregation of believers as well, a theme integral to St Paul's teaching on the Church as the body of Christ: 'If one part is

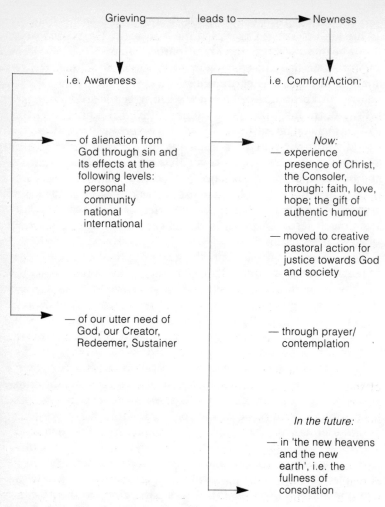

Figure 5.1 'Blessed are they who mourn . . .'

hurt, all the parts share its pain' (1 Cor 12:26). He learnt this startling lesson of corporate unity on his conversion: 'I am Jesus, whom you are persecuting' (Acts 9:5). So he berates the believers at Corinth for not grieving as a congregation because of the sins of immorality of its members (1 Cor 5:2). The community is so full of its own worldly self-importance and smugness that it is losing the sense of sin and an awareness of the need for God's saving grace; 'your self-satisfaction', he writes, 'is ill founded' (5:6).[3]

Our description of the true Christian is incomplete if we emphasize only reflection on loss in mourning. Those who mourn, says Jesus, are to be called blessed, not precisely because of their sorrow for sin, but because of what it *produces*, namely, that they 'shall be comforted' (Mt 5:5). The ultimate comfort promised is the consolation that will come from sharing in the life of the kingdom of God in its fullness, when God 'will wipe away all tears from their eyes; there will be no more death, and no more mourning or sadness or pain' (Rev 21:4).

These words from the Book of Revelation are not a mere repetition of the prophecy of Isaiah about the consolation in some indefinite future time (25:8), because the Holy Spirit is already working *now* within us to bring about its realization. This new consoling life begins at baptism where we share in Christ's triumph over the powers of chaos: 'If we have been joined to him by dying a death like his, so we shall be by a resurrection like his' (Rom 6:5).

St Paul in the same letter to the Romans again speaks of the immediate solace arising if one mourns in hope. He writes that at the present moment even we 'who have the first-fruits of the Spirit . . . are groaning inside ourselves, waiting with eagerness for our bodies to be set free. In hope, we already have salvation.' With this hope, he says, 'all that we suffer in the present time is nothing in comparison with the glory which is destined to be disclosed for us' (8:23, 18). That is, the Christian becomes sorrowful on looking at the world of sin and denial, but is immediately comforted because true happiness will come in the 'new heavens and a new earth'. The fullness of peace is anticipated *now* through hope.

The evangelist Luke refers several times to *weeping*. For example, in his list of beatitudes and curses Christ says: 'Blessed are you who are who are weeping now: you shall laugh' (6:21); 'Alas for you who are laughing now: you shall mourn and weep' (6:25). Those who weep are people who trust in God, for they weep for their sins. Those who do not weep now will do so at the end of time when God reveals his power and majesty; though they will weep then, it will be too late for their arrogance will have condemned them to eternal death.

In order to understand why Luke uses the word 'laugh' in

two different senses in the beatitudes, we need to go back to the Old Testament. Often in the Old Testament people are depicted as laughing, but it does not necessarily point to a genuine gift of humor. Rather, it is often synonymous with an expression of cruel, uncharitable, cynical, or sarcastic thoughts or speech. Abraham and Sarah both laugh at Yahweh's promise of a son (Gen 17:17; 18:12). It is a sarcastic laughter, springing from a lack of deep faith in God; they assess God's promise to them in purely human terms, so God, they believe, is totally incapable of realizing his boast. People laugh cruelly at the sufferings of Job (30:1).

It is this same type of faithless laughter that Jesus is condemning; it is synonymous with an arrogant refusal to accept God as one's creator, the Lord of all creation, and Jesus as our savior: 'Alas for you who are laughing now; you shall mourn and weep' (Lk 6:25). They resist his will here on earth, are deprived of inner joy that alone comes from the Lord, and will be rejected in the life to come: 'then there will be weeping and grinding of teeth, when you see Abraham and Isaac and Jacob and all the prophets in the kingdom of God, and yourselves thrown out' (Lk 13:28).

But those who weep for, or grieve over, their sins in this life acknowledge God as their creator; their laughter is not hollow, it is genuine because it is rooted in the gift of detachment. Through detachment we experience the relativity of all created things and the ability to discern what does or does not matter. Detachment helps to place things into true perspective. So, laughter as used here by Jesus means the joy one has when one recognizes the sheer stupidity of trying to ignore God by being sinful.

This form of laughter is attributed to Yahweh on several occasions. Yahweh's laughter is an attack on pomposity and the vanities of people, as can be seen in a passage from Psalm 2 (vv. 1–4). The kings of this world are pictured plotting against Yahweh's anointed. They forget that Yahweh can see them: 'The One whose throne is in heaven sits laughing, Yahweh derides them'. Thus those who have a true sense of humor, and can genuinely laugh at themselves in consequence, are the people who admit to their own foolish efforts to be God and are quite overcome by the fact that God still loves them with an immensity of love. Nothing is more incongruous: our efforts to play God, and God's patience towards us. And the recognition of the incongruous in human behavior is at the heart of authentic humor and laughter.

Jesus is therefore saying in Luke's account that those who truly grieve over their sinfulness now—the lost opportunities to be more deeply united with the Lord and to preach his saving message—have the gift of true humor; they contrast their own stupidities with the ever-abiding love and patience of God, and this will evoke a joy and comfort beyond all human understanding.[4]

'He has sent me . . . to comfort all who mourn' (Is 61:1f.)

The prophet Isaiah foretold the Messiah's coming. He is the one who is 'to bring the news to the afflicted, to soothe the broken-hearted . . . to comfort all who mourn' (61:1f.). Jesus is the Messiah, the one who takes away the sins of the world (Mt 1:21), the '[one who] bore our sicknesses away and carried our diseases' (Mt 8:17). He does this because through an expression of unimaginable divine pathos he 'became flesh, he lived among us' (Jn 1:14). The divine pathos of the covenant days of the Old Testament, in which Yahweh freely allowed himself to suffer with his chosen people, was but a faint shadow of the way in which the Messiah was to become involved in our lives: 'I am the living bread which has come down from heaven . . . ; it is not like the bread our ancestors ate: they are dead, but anyone who eats this bread will live for ever' (Jn 6:51, 58).

When Jesus enters into the human condition by becoming flesh and blood, he inevitably experiences all the sadnesses and griefs of peoples that either reject or accept him. Either way, he is moved to comfort people and to challenge those who refuse to admit their own sinfulness and desperate need of him. Often he takes pity on the crowds and is moved to heal the sick, encouraging them to repent and grieve for their sins (Mt 14:14). There is the touching incident where Jesus heals the severely crippled woman: 'Woman, you are freed from your disability. . . . And at once she straightened up.' She is surely comforted, not just in body but in spirit, for 'she glorified God' (Lk 13:13).

The healing of the centurion's servant touchingly points to the twofold movement from authentic grief to comfort or new-

ness. The centurion, a foreigner, on entering into himself sees
his own nothingness and sinfulness: 'Sir, I am not worthy to
have you under my roof; just give the word and my servant
will be cured' (Mt 8:8). Jesus, astonished by this remarkable
honesty, comforts the centurion: 'let this be done for you, as
your faith demands' (v. 13). Jesus uses this incident to repeat
that faith, humility and repentance are at the heart of every
authentic lament: 'I tell you, in no one in Israel have I found
faith as great as this'. The Israelites who refuse to lament their
sins 'will be thrown out into the darkness outside, where there
will be weeping and grinding of teeth' (Mt 8:10, 12).

Frequently Jesus attacks particular groups of people for their
refusal to mourn. One day, when pondering on the ways in
which people were rejecting both John the Baptist and himself,
he speaks sadly of his unsuccessful efforts to call people to let
go of their false attachments to worldly ways: 'we sang dirges,
and you wouldn't cry' (Lk 7:32). He laments over 'towns in
which most of his miracles had been worked, because they
refused to repent. . . . I tell you that it will be more bearable
for Sodom on Judgement Day than for you' (Mt 11:20, 24).

Jesus rebukes with particular sharpness and sadness the
scribes and Pharisees who do not mourn because they deny
the paralysis and death of the Judaic institutions; they refuse
to let go of irrelevant or unjust Judaic religious customs. As
whitewashed tombs—all external show and no inner openness
to the Lord—they are holding back the conversion of the
people: 'you look upright, but inside you are full of hypocrisy
and lawlessness' (Mt 23:28).

Jesus on another occasion more gently highlights the denial
of the Pharisees and the irrelevancy of the institutions they
insist on maintaining. It is the incident of the Pharisee and
the tax collector who enter the temple to pray (Lk 18:9–14).
These two people are at the opposite poles of the social scale,
one at society's peak and the other a social outcast. The
Pharisee speaks with speed and with many words to the Lord;
it is as though he is petrified of silences, lest he be forced to
look behind his arrogant façade and discover his inner nothingness. The ultimate cover-up on his part is to throw into his
speech of self-congratulation the words: 'I am not like the
tax collector here'. The tax collector, on the other hand, with
downcast eyes and the beating of his breast, laments over his
sins and his own nothingness before God. He speaks only

seven words: 'God, be merciful to me, a sinner'. And Jesus then says that humility is at the very heart of all authentic mourning: 'This man . . . went home again justified; the other did not. For everyone who raises himself up will be humbled, but anyone who humbles himself will be raised up' (Lk 18:14).

Individuals and organizations committed to proclaiming the Good News can readily fall into the same trap as the Pharisee. While planning meetings and the writing of mission statements to guide future action are all important activities, we can place so much emphasis on them that we escape from the real world. The meetings, the report writing and the debates can become 'social painkillers', which skillfully prevent us from facing the reality of loss, the necessity for Christian mourning, and openness to the apostolically new. Fewer words and discussions and more quiet, faith contemplation could provide the space for the old to be farewelled, the pastorally new to emerge and be accepted!

On one occasion St Teresa of Avila writes about the difficulties of achieving the *detachment* demanded in Christian mourning: 'it is a hard thing to withdraw from ourselves and oppose ourselves (through detachment), because we are very close to ourselves and love ourselves very dearly'. There cannot be detachment without humility. These two virtues 'are inseparable':

> These are not the kinsfolk whom I counsel you to avoid: no, you must embrace them, and love them, and never be seen without them. . . . It is to possess these virtues . . . that you must labour if you would leave the land of Egypt, for, when you have obtained them, you will also obtain the manna. . . . Resolve . . . to die for Christ.[5]

Humility is truth. Through this virtue we cast aside all pretense and hypocritical self-justification, all clinging to attitudes, structures and apostolic methods that hinder or prevent the living out of Christ's life today. Either we are for Christ or we are not; we cannot be for Christ 'without giving up all' that we own (Lk 14:33). Yet, as Jesus and St Teresa remind us, the vision of ourselves as we truly are is a formidable task; it demands of us an immense openness, and without the grace of the Lord himself this is beyond our powers: 'Things that are impossible by human resources, are possible for God' (Lk 18:27).

Jesus assures us that to those who are humble and detached there comes a comfort and a peace beyond all human understanding. The humble tax collector would have left the temple with such a gift. St Peter does not know what the results of detachment will be, but Jesus describes the vitality and joy that it brings: 'there is no one who has left house, wife, brothers, parents or children for the sake of the kingdom of God who will not receive many times as much in this present age and, in the world to come, eternal life' (Lk 18:29f.).

The reactions of Jesus to the death of Lazarus may at first sight be puzzling. Jesus uses the incident to remind Martha of the paradox that though people will die, they yet can live if they believe in him (Jn 11:25f.). When he finds crowds weeping and wailing unrestrainedly around Mary and Martha he becomes angry in the same way as he did at the deathbed of Jairus' daughter (Mk 5:38f.). Why this indignation? Jesus is saddened by discovering once more the unbelief of the Jews, because they fail to accept the possibility that Jesus could awaken Lazarus from death. They grieve as unbelievers, those who have lost all hope. Reacting as he did when the mourners of Jairus' daughter ridicule him, he is angry at the failure of people to accept him as the one who heals and comforts those who truly mourn. He laments over their blindness, their arrogant self-sufficiency.[6]

On one occasion, as Jesus approaches Jerusalem, he pauses and looks out over the city; he breaks into a powerful lament, the structure of which follows the old Hebrew dirge: 'Jerusalem, Jerusalem, you that kill the prophets and stone those who are sent to you! How often have I longed to gather your children together, as a hen gathers her chicks under her wings, and you refused!' (Mt 23:37). The city should be learning from him the way of peace, but it refuses the opportunity, and ignores its own stagnant spiritual poverty and death. And its official leaders decline to lead the city in a lament for their failings and sins (Lk 19:39f.). Jesus knows that the city is to be destroyed after his death, so he grieves and openly weeps about the calamity (Lk 19:41): 'they will leave not one stone standing on another . . . because you do not recognise the moment of your visitation' (19:44).[7]

Later, Jerusalem is the scene of another distressing lament. Women of Jerusalem spontaneously wail over Jesus as he carries his cross to his death. This is the second act of anticipatory mourning by friends or strangers, the first having occurred at Bethany when a woman—to the annoyance of the host—

poured ointment over the body of Jesus. She did it, says Jesus, 'to prepare me for burial' (Mt 26:12). The reaction of Jesus to the wailing of the Jerusalem women, however, is particularly significant. Jesus knows that through his crucifixion he will live, but those who now mourn for him are really on the threshold of destruction. So he forbids them to mourn for him, and instead invites them to grieve for themselves and for their children; they and their leaders are failing to grasp the meaning of the call to repent, which is at the heart of all true mourning (Lk 23:28).[8]

These laments are models for those who look with sadness at the denial they see in apostolic organizations, like parishes or religious congregations, to which they themselves have become devoted over time. The organizations refuse to recognize their death and they deny the need for the faith and the hope of the centurion; they will not fall on their knees before the Lord, admit the blessings and failings of the past, their fears of the future, their inadequacies to cope with needed change, their need for divine help in order to be open to new ways of preaching the Good News. They say: 'no, all is well; it is business as usual! Perhaps a little improvement of apostolic methods here or there is all that is needed to keep the organization ticking along.' Let those, however, who do mourn such blindness and stubbornness take heart from the grieving example of Jesus. Let them not feel ashamed in their sadness, anger, and loneliness, for they have in Jesus one who understands. As he prayed, let them pray from the depths of their own anguish and draw hope from the power of his Spirit.

'A man of sorrows, familiar with suffering' (Is 53:3)

Jesus fulfilled the prophecy of Isaiah to be our Consoler not just by comforting the repentant, healing the blind and the sick, but above all by *becoming* grief itself. He acquired the title of *the Consoler* (Is 51:12) by his self-humiliation, self-forgetfulness, self-emptying, filial obedience to the Father, showing no anxiety to shed the dignity of God (Ph 2:5–11). In the suffering and death of Jesus we have the model for all who mourn the loss of security, even their own lives, for the sake of the Good News: 'The Father loves me, because I lay down my life in order to take it up again . . . I lay it down of my own free will' (Jn 10:17f.).

The agony in the Garden of Gethsemane marks the first or

separation phase of the greatest of all social dramas and rituals of mourning: the agony, death, and resurrection of Christ. Jesus is both that which is to be mourned and the ritual leader at the same time.

The separation stage of a mourning ritual is characterized, as we have seen in Chapter 2, by reactions like fear, anxiety, and numbness to actual or anticipated loss; after the example of the lament psalmists, Jesus does not camouflage or deny the sufferings he is to experience. Thus the evangelist Mark records that as Jesus begins to pray he feels 'terror and anguish' (14:34), but the English translation simply cannot convey the power of the Greek text; words like 'horrified', 'shocked' or 'desolated' are still too weak to grasp what Mark is trying to say.[9] The evangelist Luke also highlights the intensity of the agony of Jesus, when he describes him praying with such earnestness that 'his sweat fell to the ground like great drops of blood' (22:44). The dramatic nature of the emotional reaction is further accentuated by the fact that, when Jesus foretold his death previously, only his disciples had expressed anxiety and desolation (Mk 8:32 and 10:32). Confrontation with the immediate harsh reality of death now evokes in Christ *himself* the powerful emotions of horror and fear.

Yet it is not only the anticipation of his suffering and death soon to overtake him that causes such distress. The enormity of the sins of the world and the way in which they alienate us from the loving concern of the Father weigh heavily upon him (Gal 2:17); he recognizes with more incisiveness than before the meaning of his mission of loving obedience and service to the Father. He begs the Father to take 'this cup away from' him (Mk 14:36). The 'cup' is an Old Testament expression for punishment and retribution of God on his people, and so here it means the burden of human sin that must be purged through his act of love.

The involvement of Satan as the tempting agent throughout his passion exacerbates his feeling of fear and loneliness. Earlier in the wilderness Satan severely tempts Jesus to refuse his role as the Servant of the Lord, but Jesus resists and he must withstand several more onslaughts. Jesus is aware that Satan's attacks are bound to return when the Father asks that he finally fulfill his mission (Jn 12:31).[10]

An additional cause for his sadness is the failure by the disciples to remain alert and at prayer with him, despite several pleas for their help. Peter is admonished by Jesus, especially because a short time before he had proudly proclaimed that 'Even if all fall away, I will not' (Mk 14:30). He who was so prepared to die for Jesus lacks the strength to watch one hour with him. Jesus reminds Peter that the Father offers him the grace of detachment so that he can be of service to his Master in his hour of need. Peter must decide between this gift and the world. He chooses the latter and once more fails (Mk 14:37–41).

We strain with little success to find the language to depict for ourselves something of the suffering and isolation of Jesus in grief in the garden. Perhaps the description that St John of the Cross, the master of dark-night purifications, gives of the loving soul called to a more intense purification by God may offer us a glimmer of what Jesus feels in the garden:

> . . . God divests the faculties, affections and senses, both spiritual and sensory, interior and exterior. He leaves the intellect in darkness, the will in aridity, the memory in emptiness and the affections in supreme affliction, bitterness and anguish, by depriving the soul of the feeling and satisfaction it previously obtained from spiritual blessings.[11]

Despite the loneliness and darkness, Jesus prays to the Father with a vigorous trust and hope that he will intervene to help him, according to the format to be found in lament psalms. The spirit of detachment remains throughout the text: 'let your will be done, not mine' (Lk 22:42).

The Father does console the Abandoned One and this is symbolized in the account of the coming of an angel 'to give him strength' (Lk 22:43). Having prayed, Jesus is strengthened to accept his death for our sins in a fully conscious way. Now there is a freshness and a vitality in his actions that contrasts markedly with his earlier fear. He knows what the Father wishes of him, so he tells his sleeping disciples to wake up and come with him to face the betrayal. On his own initiative Jesus asks the guards who they are searching for and then informs them he is the one they want (Jn 18:4–6).

The *liminal* stage of the ritual of our redemption is Christ's crucifixion and death. The scene is in many ways similar to that in the garden: Jesus deliberately moves to complete his earthly work to fulfill the Father's wishes to the end, and the tragedy continues in an atmosphere of abandonment by most of his friends. All is done with a supreme spirit of detachment and humility. He requests a final drink to assuage his thirst and this is seen by the evangelist John, through his reference back to Old Testament imagery (Ps 69:21), as a reminder to us that Jesus is consciously accepting the pain of death (Jn 19:28).[12]

The symbols of abandonment or loneliness are graphic: the words of Jesus himself, darkness, the presence of the tempter, and the disbelief of most surrounding his cross. About the ninth hour, Matthew records (27:46), Jesus cries out in anguish, yet with an abiding trust in the Father, using the opening words of the lament Psalm 22: 'My God, my God, why have you forsaken me?' Surely this is one of the most compelling of all the Old Testament songs, for here the psalmist is pictured as sinking into the uttermost chasm of suffering and despair. Reflect on these lines in which the psalmist struggles to express his desolate state and suffering, an apt description also of Jesus on the cross:

> My bones are all disjointed . . .
> My mouth is dry as earthenware,
> my tongue sticks to my jaw.
> You lay me down in the dust of death (14f.).

Battered almost to lifelessness, the psalmist turns to Yahweh to save his life. He does not ask for vengeance upon those who persecute him, but only for Yahweh's aid, who alone can restore him to health and the community. The Lord hears his frantic plea for his agony and isolation to leave him; so powerful is the Lord's intervention that the psalmist calls on the whole believing community to praise Yahweh: 'The whole wide world will remember and return to Yahweh, all the families of nations bow down before him' (v. 27).[13]

While the psalm's phrases prophetically describe the suffering of Jesus, they also point to the world-wide redemptive/renewing potential of his sacrifice. Paradoxically, it is the darkness that covers 'all the land until the ninth hour' (Mt 27:45) that may be a sign to Jesus of the Father's comforting consolation. As Yahweh created a plague of thick darkness over Egypt for three days to illustrate his sovereign power over the elements of the world (Ex 10:22f.), so now the evangelist Matthew refers to a similar God-inspired awesome darkness during the moments of the extreme suffering and death of Jesus. The old world is coming to an end, the new is being born.

Jesus himself had earlier foretold the chaos at the end of the world when 'the sun will be darkened, the moon will not give its light' (Mt 24:29). Matthew and the early Christian believers see the death/resurrection scene as the precursor of this event, and thus describe the happening here in similar language.[14]

The sense of abandonment that Jesus experiences is exacerbated by the manner in which most bystanders, including the chief priests, scribes and elders of the people, behave. They phrase their mocking questions after the manner of the tempter who earlier (Mt 4:3, 6) had tried to snatch power from Jesus: 'If you are God's son . . . come down from the cross!' (Mt 27:39). Jesus, as before, trusts in the Father and he will not give way to such arrogant taunting. The bystanders on the other hand refuse to trust in God; therefore they insist on *immediate* proof that God is present. They fail to see that at these worst moments of desolation God is most vitally present.[15]

The actual description of the death of Jesus—both priest and victim in the ritual of our redemption—is extremely brief, almost an anti-climax after the tragic drama of his suffering: ' "It is fulfilled"; and bowing his head he gave up his spirit' (Jn 19:30). Here is Jesus totally and freely giving of himself to the Father. The gesture of 'bowing his head' means that Jesus is now at peace, because his life's purpose has been accomplished and accepted by the loving Father.[16] All that now remains is the triumph of his resurrection, which is the reaggregation phase of the redemptive ritual:

> But he emptied himself . . . becoming as human beings are; . . .
> He was humbler yet, even to accepting death, death on a cross.
> And for this God raised him high . . . so that all beings in the
> heavens, on earth and in the underworld, should bend the knee
> at the name of Jesus (Ph 2:7–10).

The Gospels portray various signs that follow the death of Jesus. The temple veil tears apart 'from top to bottom' (Mk 15:38), but this is a literary artifice of the evangelizer to emphasize that with Jesus' death we are now able to approach God directly 'by a new way', namely, through the flesh and blood of Jesus our Savior (Heb 10:19–21). This is the *newness* that immediately comes from the death of Jesus.

The evangelist Matthew writes of the earth quaking, boulders splitting apart, bodies of saints rising from their tombs after the resurrection of Jesus: they 'came out of the tombs, entered the holy city and appeared to a number of people' (Mt 27:53). Again, this is a literary device of the evangelist, who wants to make a strong contrast between the death of the old and the birth of the new as a result of Christ's death and resurrection. Jesus is the first to rise from the dead in the new covenant, but we also will follow him when the present world ceases. The raising of 'bodies of the saints' dramatically symbolizes the fulfillment of the new 'life that will be ours at the end of time, when 'the sky will dissolve in flames and the elements melt in the heat' (2 Pet 3:12). We also will be raised from the dead and united with Christ in 'the new heavens and new earth, where uprightness will be at home' (2 Pet 3:13).[17]

From death to life, from renunciation to comfort—Christ sets the pattern for authentic mourning for all time. There simply can never be life for any individual or group without a dying to that which is irrelevant or an obstacle to the carrying out of the mission of the Father in Christ: 'Make your own the mind of Christ Jesus!' (Ph 2:5). Detachment is humanly costly and without the abiding support of the Holy Spirit, it is impossible to achieve. We evangelizers will use human aids, for example the skills provided by the social sciences and management studies, that help us to improve our apostolic effectiveness. However, of themselves these aids are useless *unless* we are prepared to learn detachment through grieving in union with Christ suffering, dying and rising. Only through the gift of detachment will we be prepared to give up what no longer serves the mission of the Lord and be open to the new, the apostolically creative. The challenge is frightening, but there can be no human shortcut to achieve apostolic individual or corporate resurrection: 'Here is a saying that you can rely on: If we have died with him, then we shall live with him. If we persevere, then we shall reign with him' (2 Tim 2:11) (see Figure 5.1 on p. 90).

'Near the cross of Jesus stood his mother' (Jn 19:25)

Mary is the first believer and disciple of Jesus. One senses in her pilgrimage an echo of the orientation–dislocation–reorientation ritual pattern we see in the journey of her Son. Her *orientation* stage as a simple Jewish girl with an upbringing typical of that time is shattered, when she is invited to be at the special service of God.

The heavenly messenger's exalted language implies that, as with the great people of Old Testament times, Mary is being chosen by God to do extraordinary things for him.[18] This form of address would have been enough to startle her, quite independent of the nature of the message that the angel was to give her of mothering the Son of God (Lk 1:35). Mary in faith accepts the Divine commission, and the understanding of what this challenge involves will grow over the years through her participation in several startling events. These happenings will demand from her an ever-deepening faith and detachment.

The *dislocating* or *disorientating* experience for Mary after the annunciation is her visit to Elizabeth, who is pregnant despite her advanced age, just as the angel had told her. Elizabeth praises Mary not only because she is to be the mother of Jesus, but in particular because Mary believes. She is the first disciple through faith of the yet-to-be-born Jesus. The thanksgiving hymn of Mary is a song of the oppositional themes of death/newness; the one who dies to his or her own selfish needs and lives for the Lord can do great things for God (Lk 1:46–55).

Following the birth of Jesus is the prophecy by Simeon about Mary (Lk 2:33–35), that brings a new 'low' in the dislocating process. The tone is ominous because the child is to be a cause of bitterness and division throughout Israel; there is to be much suffering *before* there is peace, and Mary is to share in this. The first painful experience of this suffering for Mary occurs when she and Joseph find the young Jesus in the temple. The puzzlement that she shows in trying to understand the independent behavior of Jesus illustrates that she has much yet to learn about her son's role, and considerable sorrow to experience in the process (Lk 2:41–50). There is a mother's anguish or pain in her rebuke to her son: 'My child, why have you done this to us? See how worried your father and I have been' (Lk 2:48). Little wonder that Mary needs time and space to ponder the meaning of this event for her son and herself. The peace of a small family circle has been lost because of her son's unforeseen and precocious behavior; this must be grieved over, if Mary is to be open to what God is to ask of her next.

There are two recorded very similar events in which Mary is praised publicly for her faith-founded obedience to the word

of God.[19] In one incident a woman from a gathering praises
Mary for having such an eloquent son, but Jesus goes much
further than that in reply. He proclaims Mary blessed since
she listens to the word of God and keeps it (Lk 11:27–28); she
is again affirmed in the role of being his first disciple in faith.[20]
Mary, like all mothers, would have experienced the normal
sadness as she watches her son grow and move away from
dependency on her; she must learn to allow him to grow and
be about his Father's business. This demands renunciation on
her part and her son congratulates her for this, and sets her
up as an example of all who mourn loss in their lives.

The greater the lover the greater the suffering in loss. And
no one loved her son more than Mary. Poets, artists and
mystics have tried for centuries to portray the grief of the
suffering mother at the foot of the cross. Some have taken the
words of the First Lamentation, in which Israel describes its
own grief at the destruction of Jerusalem by the Babylonians,
and applied them to Mary: 'All you who pass this way, look
and see: is any sorrow like the sorrow inflicted on me. . . ?'
(v. 12). Then there is the deeply inspiring thirteenth-century
hymn of grief, the *Stabat Mater*:

> At the cross her station keeping
> stood the mournful Mother weeping,
> close to Jesus to the last;
> through her heart, his sorrow sharing,
> all his bitter anguish bearing,
> now at length the sword had passed . . .
> Christ above in torments hangs;
> she beneath beholds the pangs
> of her dying glorious Son.[21]

The scene, as simply depicted by the evangelist John, is itself
forceful in its symbolism and meaning. Mary at the wedding
feast at Cana is concerned about the embarrassment to her
hosts, if it becomes known that there is no more wine. Jesus
listens to her pressing petition for help and changes the water
into wine. Because of Mary's intercession Jesus for the first
time reveals his glory and his disciples learn to believe in him
(cf. Jn 2:1–12); Mary is presented by John as symbolizing all
those people who yearn or beg for salvation through Jesus.

At the foot of the cross Mary again stands beside her son
as a symbol of all who yearn to learn self-renunciation or

detachment that they might grieve over sin with him. Now Jesus offers Mary to individuals and communities of believers throughout history, not just as an intercessor, but as a living memory of how much he loves us,[22] a love tested through suffering and death: 'Jesus said to his mother, "Woman, this is your son". Then to the disciple he said, "This is your mother" ' (19:27). In the midst of her lament of bitter anguish she is offered a new role; she is to be the support and model of detachment for every Gospel community seeking to love him and to mourn over its own sinfulness and failings:

> Let me mingle tears with you,
> mourning him who mourned for me
> all the days that I may live.[23]

When Mary is assigned to the care of the disciple John, she 'becomes most nearly conformed' to the detachment of her son, writes Hans von Balthasar. As he is 'the one sent away and abandoned by the Father', so he 'leaves her standing', sent away; he 'settles her someplace else'.[24]

The resurrection of Jesus marks for Mary the *reorientation* phase of her involvement in the ritual salvation. Renewed in faith by the triumph of her son over death and sin, Mary now helps to sustain the faith of the small group of believers as they prepare for the coming of the Holy Spirit (Acts 1:14). The coming of the Holy Spirit marks the ending of the reorientation phase for Mary: the Church is born, Mary remains the first exemplar of how we as individuals and communities are to follow Jesus in faith, hope, and love, mourning over our own sins and the sins of the world.

Summary

At one point in Luke Jesus condemns those who refuse to grieve in this world, despite all that he has done to call them to this: 'we sang dirges, and you wouldn't cry' (Lk 7:32). We cannot be authentic Christians, if we refuse constantly to grieve over our sinful attachments to what does not belong to Christ.

Christ's life, especially in his agony, death, and resurrection, is a journey of grieving, in which he is that which is lost and the leader of the mourning ritual at the same time. Detachment, which is the letting go of all that would hinder individuals or organizations from a committed relationship with God, is at the heart of all authentic grieving. Jesus is *the* model of detachment, for 'he emptied himself, taking the form of a slave . . . accepting death, death on a cross' (Ph 2:7, 8), in order that we might share the new fruits of his victory over death through his resurrection: 'In all truth I tell you, you will be weeping and wailing while the world will rejoice; you will be sorrowful, but your sorrow will turn to joy' (Jn 16:20).

Discussion questions

1. What does St Paul mean when he writes: 'We want you to be quite certain . . . about those who have fallen asleep, to make sure that you do not grieve for them, as others who have no hope' (1 Th 4:13)? For example, does St Paul mean we should not grieve at all?
2. Why is detachment at the heart of authentic Christian mourning?
3. Read the stories about 'the lost sheep', 'the lost drachma', and 'the lost son and the dutiful son' in chapter 15 of St Luke's Gospel. What do they teach us about the grieving process? (Members of the group may like to re-read Chapters 1 and 2 above before answering this question.)
4. What is meant by the statement that 'those who have a Gospel sense of humor also possess the gift of grieving'?

References

1. For examples see Pss 41:1; 65:4; 84:5; 106:3; 112:1.
2. See B. W. Anderson, *Creation Versus Chaos: The Reinterpretation of Mythical Symbolism in the Bible* (New York: Association Press, 1967), pp. 160–70.
3. See R. Bultmann in G. Friedrich (ed.), *Theological Dictionary of the New Testament* (Grand Rapids, MI: W. B. Eerdmans, 1968), vol. 6, pp. 42f.
4. See G. A. Arbuckle, *Strategies for Growth in Religious Life* (New York: Alba House, 1986), pp. 67–87; K. H. Rengstorf in G. Kittel (ed.), *Theological Dictionary of the New Testament* (Grand Rapids, MI: W. B. Eerdmans, 1965), vol. 3, pp. 722–6.
5. Trans. E. A. Peers, *The Complete Works of St Teresa of Jesus* (London: Sheed & Ward, 1946), pp. 43f.
6. See C. K. Barrett, *The Gospel According to St John: An Introduction with Commentary and Notes on the Greek Text* (London: SPCK, 1978), pp. 398–401; R. Schnackenburg, *The Gospel According to St John* (London: Burns & Oates, 1980), pp. 334–8.

7. See I. H. Marshall, *The Gospel of Luke: A Commentary on the Greek Text* (Exeter: Paternoster Press, 1978), pp. 717–19.
8. See G. Stahlin in G. Kittel (ed.), *Theological Dictionary of the New Testament* (Grand Rapids, MI: W. B. Eerdmans, 1965), vol. 3, pp. 152–5; and Rengstorf, ibid., p. 725.
9. With the possible exception of the anger of Jesus at the faithless mourning of people at the death of Lazarus (Jn 11:33–38). See D. M. Stanley, *Jesus in Gethsemane* (New York: Paulist Press, 1980), p. 132; and V. Taylor, *The Gospel According to St Mark* (London: Macmillan, 1955), pp. 552–6.
10. See C. E. B. Cranfield, *The Gospel According to Saint Mark* (Cambridge, UK: Cambridge University Press, 1979), pp. 431f.
11. Trans. K. Kavanaugh and O. Rodriguez, *The Collected Works of Saint John of the Cross* (Washington, DC: Institute of Carmelite Studies, 1973), bk 2, ch. 2 [Dark Night].
12. See R. Schnackenburg, *The Gospel According to St John* (London: Burns & Oates, 1982), vol. 3, pp. 283ff.
13. See A. Weiser, *The Psalms: A Commentary* (London: SCM Press, 1962), pp. 219–26.
14. See D. P. Senior, *The Passion of Jesus in the Gospel of Matthew* (Wilmington, DE: Michael Glazier, 1985), pp. 135–50.
15. Ibid., pp. 298f.
16. See Schnackenburg, *The Gospel According to St John*, op. cit., p. 284.
17. See I. H. Marshall, *The Gospel of Luke: A Commentary on the Greek Text* (Exeter: Paternoster Press, 1978), p. 66.
18. See J. P. Meier, *Matthew* (Dublin: Veritas Publications, 1980), pp. 351f.
19. See J. A. Fitzmyer, *The Gospel According to Luke (I–IX)* (New York: Doubleday, 1981), pp. 422f.
20. See J. A. Fitzmyer, *The Gospel According to Luke (X–XXIV)* (New York: Doubleday, 1985), pp. 926–9.
21. 'Stabat Mater' in *Lectionary* (London: Collins/Geoffrey Chapman, 1983), p. 1126.
22. See Schnackenburg, *The Gospel According to St John*, op. cit., vol. 3, pp. 274–82; J. A. Grassi, *Mary: Mother and Disciple* (Wilmington, DE: Michael Glazier, 1988), pp. 76–88.
23. 'Stabat Mater', op. cit.
24. M. Kehl and W. Loser (eds), *The Von Balthasar Reader* (Edinburgh: T. & T. Clark, 1985), pp. 324f.

PART THREE

Initiating the Grieving Process

Let sorrow lend me words, and words express
The manner of my pity-wanting pain
(Shakespeare, *Sonnets*, no. cxi).

Chapter 6

DEATH AND NEWNESS IN EARTHING THE GOSPEL

Let the earth produce every kind of living creature . . . (Gen 1:24).

Those who sow in tears sing as they reap (Ps 126:5).

In previous chapters the examples of loss mostly stress how individuals, groups, and institutions—such as parishes, religious congregations, mission societies—must mourn as a result of changes that affect them from *outside*. People or organizations are in a sense passive receivers of loss; they do not deliberately encourage a state of individual or corporate bereavement. I have argued that this experience of loss requires that we undergo grieving processes in ways clearly prescribed in the Old and New Testaments; at the heart of these rituals of grief is a spirituality of detachment.

However, there are other forms of loss that people feel, because they are actively involved in initiating evangelization projects. Rather than having loss imposed on them from outside, individuals and communities committed to evangelization deliberately *foster* it in order to be able to respond more positively to the ever-changing pastoral needs of the world. This chapter is about these latter types of loss and the importance for all who preach the Gospel—be they individuals, organizations, cultures—to nurture a spirituality of letting go. We will look in further depth at the insight that detachment and rituals of grief apostolically necessitate not just a letting go of the past, but a process of receiving as well. Mourning is a dynamic exchange movement.

First, an explanation of the meaning of evangelization as referred to in the previous paragraph. Evangelization is here synonymous with what is called today *inculturation* (or by some, *contextualization*). I will define inculturation, explain its scriptural foundation, and then offer a series of short case studies to illustrate what the spirituality of inculturation or detachment/exchange involves.[1]

Defining inculturation

Inculturation is the dynamic interrelationship 'between the Christian message and culture or cultures; an insertion of the Christian life into a culture; an ongoing process of reciprocal and critical interaction and assimilation between them'.[2] Inculturation is the process of evangelization whereby cultures are elevated and purified through interaction with the Gospel message. What is good within a culture receives the further affirmation of the Gospel and is offered to God as an additional testimony of his goodness. Some brief comments on the definition:

1. The object of evangelization

The object of evangelization is not directly the individual, but this or that particular culture. This is the meaning of the following quotation from Pope Paul VI:

> [Cultures] have to be regenerated by an encounter with the Gospel. . . . What matters is to evangelize our culture and cultures (not in a purely decorative way as it were by applying a thin veneer, but in a vital way, in depth and right to their very roots) . . . always taking the person as one's starting-point and always coming back to the relationships of people among themselves and with God.[3]

At first this might sound surprising, since we are accustomed to hear that evangelization is concerned with the conversion of this or that person. However, the reality is that no one can live without a culture, with its network of common symbols, myths, and rituals that give meaning and significance to the lives of individuals. A culture permeates every fibre of a person's being; by seeking to evangelize a culture one is aiming to provide an atmosphere in which the individual can more easily and freely turn to the Lord in justice and love. If a culture remains contrary to Gospel principles, then people are being oppressed by attitudes and structures of injustice. In such a culture of oppression it is extremely difficult, if not impossible, for people to become the agents of their own growth; we have seen in Chapter 4 that the prophets in Old Testament times severely criticized cultures of oppression in which the powerful and wealthy ruled for their own advantage.

The term 'inculturation' was invented in the 1970s to emphasize the fact that the Gospel must penetrate into the very heart of a culture—that is, into the ways people feel, think and act. This is what is meant by the term 'insertion' in the definition. So, inculturation does not mean that evangelization is to be concerned only with the structures/institutions or the visible expressions/customs of a culture; rather, it is to interact especially with the inner values and feelings of people.

2. Encounter between two cultures

The process of evangelization is not a simple encounter between the culturally 'untainted' New Testament and a particular culture, because the Gospel comes down to us as already embedded in the particular culture of the time of the evangelists. An ongoing discernment is required to discover what is at the heart of Christ's message, and what belongs to Hebrew/Greek languages and cultures of his time and that of the evangelists. Since St Paul, for example, lived in a thoroughly patriarchal culture, his commentary on the obedience of the wife to the husband and the slave to the master must be read with this cultural background in mind.

There is a further complication, because over the centuries explanations of the Gospel truths have often become encrusted with European ways of thinking and acting. So peoples in Asia and elsewhere have frequently received the Gospel message with the unnecessary additions of Eurocentric expressions and interpretations. Inculturation demands that Gospel truths be also purged of these accretions.

3. Inculturation: a process of exchange

Inculturation is a process of exchange[4] or 'reciprocal and critical interaction and assimilation between' the Gospel and culture(s). This exchange takes place at several levels.

First, not only is there a giving to a culture on the part of the Gospel, but there is also a receiving in return. In a sense, the Gospel is 'changed' through contact with cultures. New insights into the message of Christ can be obtained as the evangelizer listens to, and is questioned by, the people being evangelized. For example, through contact with cultures of the poor in South America, theologians have been able to sharpen our understanding of Jesus in the Gospels as the Liberator of the marginalized.

Second, the evangelizing person or culture also receives as well as gives to other cultures/subcultures, be they youth, old-age, ethnic, or any other type of culture. This contradicts the experience of the last few centuries within the Church. It was often uncritically assumed that the evangelizer had nothing significant to learn from the people or cultures being evangelized. Few ever believed that the Holy Spirit is active in all cultures, even before they make contact with the Gospel. This assumption of superiority cultivated a missionary arrogance and paternalism, and even at times a violent fanaticism in our one-sided presentation of the Good News.

So, the inculturation ethic requires that we evangelizers take time to understand as fully as possible the peoples and cultures we are evangelizing. We are to do this not simply in order to be able to *use* their customs as better vehicles to explain the faith, but as avenues to discover the marvelous and divers ways in which people are responding to the graces offered them by the Lord. After all, the evangelizer, who through his or her skill helps a culture to respond to its desire to know Christ better, is the one who gains most of all. Riches of faith and insight of a very special kind are received in return for the evangelizer's efforts and are part of the hundredfold promised to those who love the Lord. Of course, this necessitates that we admit through a process of grieving that our own culture and knowledge of the ways of the Lord are limited. It requires a spirit of detachment to put aside our own culture-centered sense of superiority.

An example will illustrate what I mean. In the mid-1960s I was researching the impact of credit unions (small-scale, people-owned bank and loan societies) on village life in the South Pacific islands of Fiji. At the beginning of the research I was especially conscious of my own highly educated background. I did not believe that the islanders had anything particularly important to offer me, and certainly nothing about the dignity of the human person and how people can grow through assuming responsibility for themselves and others. One of my first interviews was with a very poorly educated elderly islander and I rather paternalistically asked him what he had received from his local credit union. He answered:

> For the first time in my life, I felt trusted as a person. All my life people had been saying to Fijians like me that we are worthless people, not to be trusted with money and the management of our own affairs. I was given a loan on the basis of my character alone. This was the very first time that people had trusted me. They believed that I would pay back the loan through my own efforts. When they trusted me, then I discovered that I was something worthwhile. I could stand up with my head high, just like other people. I think this is what Jesus meant when he said he had come to liberate prisoners. I had been, with so many other Fijians, prisoners of our poor self-image. My family could be proud of me at last.

This reply startled me. I suddenly realized that this man knew from personal experience far more than I did about human dignity and how it is to be realized. In his own way he had depthed a fundamental dimension of Christ's mission: the liberation of the powerless, the marginalized. My knowledge was from books; his was from long, bitter, personal, and cultural experience of suffering under a paternalistic colonial government.

The incident continues to influence me. It teaches me this difficult lesson: that I must continue always to struggle to listen to people at all levels of society, especially the poorest. Then I can continue to discover the marvelous ways in which the Spirit works in people's lives and what the Lord means when he speaks of his special love for the oppressed of this world. This gift of listening to others does not come easily to me, because it means that I must be ever begging the Lord for the grace of letting go of my own sense of exalted self-importance.

4. Evangelizers do not inculturate: people do

Individuals in and through their communities of faith initiate and carry through the process of inculturation. So we read that individual Churches, intimately built up not only of people but of particular ways of feeling, thinking, and acting have the task of assimilating the Gospel message in ways that are uniquely understandable to them. The structures of government, the ways of worship, and teaching the Gospel will differ from culture to culture, though the substance of the faith will remain the same throughout the world.[5]

In practical terms this means that inculturation does not occur simply because an evangelizer tells people how the Gospel is to be lived out in their particular cultural setting. In other words, inculturation is not the unique task of an intellectual, evangelizing or theological elite that decides within the rarefied atmosphere of libraries, universities, rectories, or conferences what inculturation should mean for this or that group of people. It is a *co-operative* process. People at all levels of a community must be involved in the process, for the Holy Spirit is active within all of us, as St Paul reminds us on several occasions (Rom 12:6–8; 1 Cor 12:1–30).

This means that theological and pastoral experts must restrain their enthusiasm to jump in and tell people just what inculturation should mean for them. They can only do this if they have a spirit of Gospel detachment. They must learn to grieve over their loss of the control derived from having training that others do not possess and develop an openness to learn from the experience of people far less educated than themselves. The newness they will discover is the richness of the experience of others and the power of the Holy Spirit working in their lives. No theological textbook can teach them this!

Finally, the decision to act according to Gospel insights in a particular cultural setting does not in itself constitute inculturation. Only in the actual application of the Gospel insights to life does inculturation occur, and conversion is necessary for this to take place. Talk, no matter how eloquent and learned it may be, without conversion is not inculturation.

5. Inculturation is obeying the Lord

To obey means in both Testaments to hear and to do. Thus Moses is told by Yahweh that 'If you listen carefully to the voice of Yahweh your God and do what he regards as right . . . I shall never inflict on you any of the diseases' (Ex 15:26). The entire life of Jesus is a process of listening to his Father and then acting. When Peter tries to stop Jesus from following the way of suffering, Jesus berates him as a tempter, and asserts that it is not the words of humans that he must hear and obey, but those of the Father (Mk 8:33). The prayer at

Gethsemane illustrates to what depths of suffering his listening to the will of the Father leads him (Mk 14:36). Throughout his life Jesus yearns to discover the Father's will and often we see him withdrawing to pray in order to hear without distraction what is being asked of him.

For the evangelizer, therefore, inculturation means precisely what the words 'to listen' connote in the Scriptures. In order to know what the Lord is asking to be done, the individual or community must seek to hear God speaking to them in their prayerful reflection on the Scriptures, in the events of their own lives, and in the pastoral needs around them. And having listened, they must act. Then inculturation is taking place.

The incarnation: the foundation/model of all inculturation

Inculturation is a process or ritual of mourning; that is, it is a movement whereby we let go whatever does not foster Gospel life and we open our hearts to whatever facilitates this life within ourselves and the world in which we live. The theology and spirituality behind this assertion is based on the example and teaching of Christ himself, as the previous chapter has explained. However, our reflection on inculturation may be helped by first pondering further on the mystery of the incarnation. Then, secondly, we reflect on the use that Jesus makes of agricultural metaphors to explain what must happen when conversion to his message takes place.

In the prologue of John's Gospel we have in solemn and stately language the summary of the entire Good News: the divinity of the Lord, his role in the creation of the world, his entering into the very heart of the human condition to win salvation for us. One verse in particular of the prologue is the foundation of all that we mean by inculturation: 'The Word became flesh, he lived among us' (v. 4). Bruce Vawter asserts that 'This is one of the most serious and sobering statements in the Gospel, the magnitude of which it would be difficult to exaggerate'.[6] The phrase 'he lived among us' is similar to that which was used of Yahweh when he 'pitched his tent' with the Israelites in the desert (Ex 40:34f.). The tent or Tabernacle became his localized presence on the earth. But the previous phrase, 'The Word became flesh', describes a presence beyond the wildest dreams of the Israelites.

God is present to us not only as our Creator, but he becomes part of his own creation through taking on the weaknesses and limitations of being human. As St Paul says: 'What the Law could not do because of the weakness of human nature, God did, sending his own Son in the same human nature as any sinner to be a sacrifice for sin' (Rom 8:3). By becoming flesh, the Word becomes inextricably bound to human history.[7] The incarnation involves an *exchange*, the dignity and power of which it is humanly speaking impossible to grasp—only faith can give us a tiny glimpse of its reality: God becomes one of us, even to the extent that he accepts suffering and death. Through Christ we become, as it were, God, and can speak of him as our brother and his Father as our Father.

This exchange is relived every time there is an act of inculturation. God in Christ enters more fully into our human condition; we share more intimately in his life. Thus when an act of justice occurs, Jesus is a little more present within this or that culture; through an act of justice, we die with Christ to that which is sinful and we rise to a creative newness in human relationships through the transforming power of Christ. When we experience injustice, Christ also profoundly suffers with us. He suffers when a dominant culture refuses to acknowledge the rights of minority peoples, because the process of inculturation or the presence of Gospel justice is denied them—and Christ at the same time. To Paul, Jesus proclaims: 'I am Jesus, whom you are persecuting' (Acts 9:5).

Metaphors for inculturation: the earth, the sower and the seed

Jesus is a masterful teacher. He catches and keeps the attention of his listeners by telling stories that involve objects they are familiar with. And since Jews are agricultural people, Jesus quite naturally, as Old Testament writers and prophets before him, uses the images of the earth—vines, olive trees, the seed, and sower—to convey some basic truths about his kingdom and the role of evangelizers in fostering its growth.

When Jesus uses the images of seeds and sowers, he gives us deep insights into the nature of inculturation and of grieving for newness that is intimately part of its process. Jesus takes seeds to illustrate his teaching in four parables: the seed and weeds (Mt 31:24–30); the sower, seed, and soils (Mt 13:3–9); the seed growing secretly (Mk 4:26–29); and the mustard seed (Mk 4:30–32). On one occasion, Jesus uses the potential of a tiny mustard seed to develop into 'the biggest of shrubs' in order to describe what the kingdom of heaven will be like (Mt 13:31f.). The kingdom of heaven is born within the hearts of people who freely accept the seed, which is the Word of God (Lk 8:11).

In the parable of the sower and the seed Jesus particularly stresses not just the seed, but also the symbolism of the earth. The earth symbolizes the hearer of the Word of God, which is the seed. If the seed is to germinate and grow, then the earth and the seed must interact—there must be an exchange, a giving and a taking. The earth has life the seed needs if it is to sprout and grow; if the earth fails to co-operate, then the seed dies, but if the seed falls into rich, co-operating soil then the crop is a hundredfold (Lk 8:8).

We need to look a little further into the meanings that Jesus gives the earth (Mt 13:18–23). Seeds that are sown on a pathway have little chance of growing, as they are easy prey to birds. So also, says Jesus, is the human heart like the thin earth of a pathway when a person hears, but fails to absorb or internalize the Word of God. When seeds fall on rocky ground there is an immediate growth, but the plants wither away once the hot sun comes up because the soil is too thin. Likewise, the person who hears the Word of God is like the rocky ground when he or she receives it with joy, but fails to understand that the Word of God must be nourished through suffering, tribulation, and community support. Then the joy is truly Christ-like. Earlier Jesus had warned his disciples that if they truly hear the Good News, they 'will be universally hated on account' of his name for the 'disciple is not superior to teacher, nor slave to master' (Mt 10:22, 24). The seeds that fall among the thorns are eventually smothered by these thorns; the seed of faith is almost suffocated when it is received by people trying to maintain at the same time a love of the world and its riches. They are attempting to do the impossible—to be attached to two cultures at the same time: one based on the values of Jesus and the other on the denial of his Word. 'No one can be a slave of two masters', Jesus had earlier told his listeners (Mt 6:24). Cultural values contrary to the teachings of Jesus must be allowed to die.

However, the seeds that are sown in rich soil produce a fine crop. 'Rich soil' (Mt 13:23) symbolizes those people who recognize that in order to receive and live out the Word of God they must be prepared to accept rejection and per- secution. They cannot survive such suffering unless they are already committed to lives of renunciation or death-to-self.[8]

This parable can help us grasp what is meant by incultur- ation as a process of exchange. Jesus says: 'Anyone who has ears should listen' (Mt 13:9); that is, the parable has a lesson that can be grasped only through deep pondering in faith. The heart (the earth) of the hearer of the Good News must be disposed in faith to receive; having received, the hearer must then give something back to the giver—Jesus Christ. What is to be given is the hundredfold harvest of charity and justice. The process of inculturation cannot be done on behalf of some- one else nor can it be imposed on people. It is a process of faith, of personal and group conversion, of death to worldly attachments, of free receiving and giving back to the Lord.

While this parable stresses the symbolism of the interaction between the seed and the earth, Jesus in a later parable emphasizes the Gospel symbolism of the sower—that is, the evangelizer. The sower of the kingdom of heaven is first Jesus himself (Mt 13:37). Christ is the wheat grain *and* the sower. He must die if there is to be life: 'Now the hour has come . . . unless a wheat grain falls into the earth and dies, it remains only a single grain; but if it dies it yields a rich harvest' (Jn 12:23f.). All who listen to Jesus will have the power also to be a Gospel wheat-grain (1 Jn 3:9), *and* at the same time sower or evangelizer of the Good News to others; yet one cannot be an effective grain or sower unless there is death to one's own false attachments.

Following the example of Christ, we take the agricultural symbolism a little further. The evangelizer as the sower offers the seed of the Good News to a people or culture. Like all good sowers, he or she must prepare the ground, seek advice from knowledgeable people about the best time and methods to sow the seed, nurturing it when growth emerges, but avoid- ing too much care lest the young plant becomes overly depen- dent.

As the Gospel and cultures are both modified or changed

in some way or other through interaction (though the substance of the Good News remains intact), so also is the evangelizer as the sower. The good gardener is affected through
contact with the earth, for there is joy and grief at the success
and failure of earthing the seeds. The evangelizer is no different; the more he or she gives to the earthing process, the more
they are enriched through faith contact with both the culture
and the Gospel. The evangelizer sees people trying new ways
of preaching the Gospel and this challenges the evangelizer to
change or modify the long-standing customs of his or her
culture of teaching.

Our understanding of why Jesus insists on the need for the
seed and sower to die can be enriched by reference to Psalm
126. He and his listeners would be aware of this psalm. In the
opening words of the psalm the writer dreams that the nation
will struggle out of its barren exile into fields rich in peace
and hope of future blessings. Yahweh is the source of this
hope, just as he has been the strength of his people in the
past. Other nations will stand in awe at the mighty deeds of
Yahweh; Israelites must understand that Yahweh is for all
peoples. When foreigners come to bow before the returning
Israelites, they will be honoring not the nation, but Yahweh's
power that leads the people back from exile. In brief, the
meaning is: let Israel remember that its strength comes only
from God and that same power he offers to other peoples as
well (vv. 2f.). The role of true Israelites is not to return to
the evil ways of the past, but to place their absolute trust
in Yahweh; there is nothing he cannot do if they and other
peoples have faith in him.

Inspired with such faith the psalmist calls on Yahweh to
continue to lead his people out of captivity (v. 4). Yahweh
responds to this faith by assuring his covenant partners that
they will truly rejoice, but it must be prefaced with tears of
mourning:

> Those who sow in tears sing as they reap.
> He went off, went off weeping, carrying the seed.
> He comes back, comes back singing, bringing in
> his sheaves (vv. 5f.).

It was a commonly accepted agricultural custom, and Jesus
acknowledges and further develops the theme, that sowing is
to be thought of as a time of mourning; that is, there must be

grief over loss before there is new life. The Israelites see their present sufferings in exile as the time to mourn over their past failings in Yahweh's presence; God's mysterious power will draw good out of these sufferings.[9]

The lessons of this psalm further illuminate what the process of inculturation requires of evangelizers. No evangelizer can exalt his or her own culture or professional knowledge to the detriment of God's sovereign rights as the creator and sustainer of all; Jesus Christ is to be preached above everything else, not one's social status or favorite cultural way of doing or saying things. One must be prepared to let these things die to allow the Lord to take root in the hearts of other people, whose ways of acting differ from one's own profession or culture. Finally, inculturation is a *team* effort: evangelizers, those being evangelized, and the Lord himself. The Lord is the dominant figure in the process, the source of our hope and strength:

> For what is Apollos and what is Paul? . . . I did the planting, Apollos did the watering, but God gave growth. It is all one who does the planting and who does the watering. . . . After all, we do share in God's work; you are God's farm, God's building (1 Cor 3:5–9).

In inculturation cultures experience loss

Inculturation has been variously misunderstood. Sometimes it is thought to be synonymous with *nationalism*; that is, it is claimed that one's culture is to be the uncritical measure of what the Gospel means. At other times inculturation is thought to be synonymous with *acculturation*. The latter, unlike inculturation which is a theological expression, is a purely sociological term, meaning the acquisition by one society of the cultural values and customs of another society. For example, at the time of Emperor Constantine, Church officials often uncritically acculturated the secular power symbols of the imperial culture.

Two incidents recorded in the Acts of the Apostles demonstrate that inculturation can never be synonymous with nationalism or acculturation. Inculturation demands a spirit of renunciation of whatever does not belong to the Gospel. It is a never-ending process of personal and cultural dying in order to allow the Lord to reign within and around us.

The first incident relates the story of Cornelius (10:1–33), a Roman soldier stationed at Caesarea, who, while a devoted proselyte of the new Christian faith, is not a full member of the Jewish community through circumcision. Peter is summoned by an angel to visit Cornelius, but before he does that, he himself has a vision assuring him that nothing is unclean that God has purified. It is perfectly correct, in opposition to a Pharisaic law, to baptize and associate with Gentiles. When Peter had earlier followed this Pharisaic prohibition, he had been rebuked by Paul (Gal 1:12ff.), but a vision is necessary to convince Peter finally of a fundamental pastoral guideline: the Good News is the measure of cultures and not vice versa. So Cornelius is baptized and admitted into the community of believers as a social equal.

The same confusion of faith and Jewish culture also endangers the apostolic work of St Paul and others. This time several members of the Church of Jerusalem come to Antioch to demand that when Gentiles become Christians they must also adopt the Jewish culture. St Paul believes that these people are advocating the return to a form of religious and cultural slavery (Gal 2:4). It is decided that Paul and Barnabas should go up to Jerusalem and discuss the vexing 'question with the apostles and elders' in Jerusalem (Acts 15:2). There then takes place in about AD 49 what has become known as the Council of Jersualem, a major turning point in the history of the Church itself. From a primitive, Jewish-oriented community, Christianity formally becomes a Church for all cultures.

The Council 'decided by the Holy Spirit and by ourselves not to impose on' peoples of different cultures 'any burden beyond these essentials': the Gentile converts are not to be forced to accept the whole Mosaic Law, but a minimum of Jewish religious customs would still be required in areas where there are large communities of Jews (Acts 15:28f.). Jewish Christians had to be told to allow customs to die that are not part of the heart of the new faith; certainly, they must never impose them on non-Jews.[10]

Christ himself had made this point on several occasions, but it had taken a long time for the message to be understood: the need for evangelizers to allow those cultural values and customs to die that are inimical to the Gospel message. It requires, he kept saying, a gift of listening to the Good News and to one's culture in order to discern what should be maintained or renounced for the sake of the kingdom. Consider the example of the transfiguration which follows the form of a ritual process. Jesus is anxious to teach his disciples his identity and mission (Lk 9:1–27); yet they do not really listen or understand what he is saying, despite the miracles. So he invites three disciples—Peter, James and John—to leave their daily routine for a time that they might come to know him more intimately through prayer together. The journeying up the mountain we may call the separation stage of the ritual of initiation into a closer friendship with Jesus for these three chosen ones (Lk 9:28).

The liminality or dislocation experience is the actual transfiguration itself (Lk 9:29–36). A completely satisfactory answer is given by the Father himself within a rather dramatic atmosphere to the question of Jesus' identity and the nature of his mission: 'This is my Son, the Chosen One' (v. 35). These words identify Jesus not only as the Messiah, but as God's Son. It is the same Son who is 'to suffer grievously, to be rejected by the elders and chief priests and scribes and to be put to death, and to be raised up on the third day' (Lk 9:22). Moses and Elijah are present, representing the Israelite culture of old, but they disappear, leaving Jesus alone. Their departure from the scene symbolizes that Jesus must now fulfill his mission and that aspects of the Jewish faith of the old dispensation which contradict his teaching must cease to exist. The disciples are charged to listen to Jesus, the Messiah of the new covenant, thus implying that he now speaks with the authority of the Father, which is higher than any human authority, even that of Moses and Elijah from the old covenant.[11]

Peter is overcome by the scene. Neither listening nor being able to comprehend the symbolism of what is happening (v. 33), he does not want Moses and Elijah to leave. He is anxious, therefore, to build shelters for Jesus and the two Old Testament figures. Peter symbolizes here those evangelizers earnestly wanting to hold on to customs that either have lost all relevance for the preaching of the Good News, or are opposed to the message of Christ.

The reaggregation stage of the ritual of initiation for the three disciples into a deeper knowledge of Jesus and his mission begins with the journey down from the mountain (Lk 9:37). Yet, despite all that has happened, the disciples cling to Israelite cultural values about power and prestige that contradict the teachings of Jesus. They quickly dispute with each other about who is the greatest among them and 'who should be allowed to perform miracles'.[12]

The incident about an inhospitable Samaritan village (Lk 9:51–56) involving James and John after the transfiguration needs comment. It again illustrates their failure to allow cultural values to die that diverge from the teachings of Jesus. Jesus and his followers are on their way to Jerusalem and messengers are sent ahead, presumably to arrange accommodation and food, but the villagers refuse their requests. They are rejected because Samaritans have inherited racial prejudice against Jews.

James and John, angered by such rejection, are anxious that they share in the power of Jesus to work a miracle to punish the Samaritans; they wanted 'fire from heaven to burn them up' (Lk 9:54). The two disciples are aware of what Elijah, whom they have recently witnessed talking with Jesus, did to an annoying captain and fifty soldiers; he had called down fire from heaven and it destroyed them (1 Kg 1:10). Jesus then rebukes James and John, for they had not yet comprehended the fact that Jesus was establishing a new covenant in which retaliation—an eye for an eye, a tooth for a tooth—was not permissible. The disciples had not grasped at all what Jesus had earlier said about his mission (Lk 9:45), nor had the experience of the transfiguration had any impact whatsoever on them.[13]

There are lessons in this event that will always be relevant. For example, contemporary Protestant or Roman Catholic evangelizers, annoyed by the slowness of ecumenical cooperation, may be tempted to revive old sectarian prejudices. If so, they are no different from James and John because they fail to grasp the fact that the law of love, tolerance, and patience must govern the behavior of all followers of Jesus. The fostering of sectarian bitterness may give its supporters a twisted sense of power, but it has no support in the Gospels.

Jesus takes other opportunities, for example in the Good Samaritan story, to teach his followers that racial or cultural prejudice is inherently contrary to his teaching and must be cast aside as evil. In the Good Samaritan story the Samaritan is presented as an example of how his followers must love all peoples, no matter what their race, religion, or culture (Lk 10:29–37). The Jewish people consider the Samaritans to be a dangerous heretical and schismatic group to be despised even more than pagan peoples. John L. McKenzie writes that 'There was no deeper breach of human relations in the contemporary world than the feud of Jews and Samaritans, and the breadth and depth of Jesus' doctrine of love could demand no greater act of a Jew than to accept a Samaritan as a brother'.[14] The listeners to the story of Jesus are therefore left in no doubt that his message radically contradicts inherited Jewish prejudice against Samaritans.

Within most parishes today there are to be found all kinds of cultures and subcultures; for example, the subcultures of youth and old age, and divers ethnic groups. The evangelizer in proclaiming the Good News must be able to relate to them in ways that exclude all forms of prejudice. For example, contemporary society often treats the elderly as nuisances, as people who are no longer expected to have a creative idea or be responsible for decisions about their own lives. Thus, evangelizers wishing to work among the elderly must discover and root out whatever cultural prejudices exist within themselves. If they fail to do so, they will be reinforcing these prejudices to the detriment of the people they wish to serve and the proclamation of the Gospel.

REFLECTIONS ON CASE STUDIES

Case studies can provide data or a human richness and detail that the theoretical analysis such as is provided above simply cannot convey. The following are several case studies that relate how individuals/institutions cope with the losses that the commitment to inculturation inevitably involves. I would invite readers to ponder the case studies without immediately reading the commentaries that are attached. Let them see if they can recognize, in the light of the theory given in this book, the weaknesses and strengths of the people involved in the incidents as they face the challenges of inculturation. Readers may like to use check questions such as the following: Are people in the case studies sensitive in theory and in practice to the fact that inculturation demands mourning? How would *I* react in the circumstances of the case studies?

1. Initial formation for religious life
Though a religious congregation of women, founded last century in France, is dying within the Western world, nonetheless

vigorous efforts are being made to recruit candidates within the Third World. The methods of recruitment and training are causing considerable tension and conflict. On the one hand, individuals directly involved in the formation of the candidates are concerned that people are being sent them by the congregation's administrators, without adequate screening and academic preparation. When unsuitable candidates are advised to leave by the formators, the latter are severely criticized by administrators and others for their 'insensitive' judgments in ways like the following comment:

> God is being good to us in sending us vocations. The standards of acceptance must not be those of the Western world. We know the backgrounds of these people and we are confident that they will turn out good religious. We know the local people better than you and it is quite clear that you do not trust them as we do. Teach them to pray and they will do a good job in the future. Have faith! The Lord has so much work for us that he does not want us to turn away those who ask to be his apostolic servants.

Comment
The views of these administrators are dangerously paternalistic, even racist. The assumption is that the candidates within the Third World are basically different from those in the West; they belong to the non-existent 'noble savage' class, and if nurtured and constantly supervised, they will flourish and do exactly what is expected of them. The administrators have not accepted the reality of the incarnation and thus reject the fact that the Spirit speaks to us not just in the Gospels, but through events and the experience of human research. Hence, they distrust as 'a lot of nonsense' the cross-cultural research findings of contemporary psychology and anthropology about the problems and challenges of human growth. Christ asks of us not just to pray, but to work justly according to his teachings; the excessive emphasis on prayer as the solution to all problems is perilously naïve theologically, and even unjust to the candidates involved.[15]

2. The challenge of multiculturalism
A particular country is inhabited by two major cultural groups: the dominant Anglo-Saxon culture brought by colonizers last century, and a minority culture belonging to people descended from the land's original inhabitants. Anglo-Saxon members of

one parish recently concluded a series of study programs aimed at helping them understand why Christians must be committed to the apostolate of justice.

When it came to deciding on practical solutions to the injustices being suffered by people of the minority culture, the parishioners were deeply divided about what to do. One group concluded:

> The main reason why minority group persons do not come to Sunday services in our church is that they are insufficiently educated in our ways of praying. We recommend that we go out and visit them, tell them we love them in Jesus, and wish to teach them why and how they should pray with us. We would invite them to come to our church so that we could all pray in the same way and place.

A second group strongly disagreed with this approach:

> Let us ask their leaders if they would mind our visiting them. We would offer to pray with them where *they* live. In our prayers we would ask their forgiveness for the arrogance of our people over the last hundred years towards them. We would ask them if they could help us to learn to pray in their way.

Comment

The concern among Anglo-Saxon parishioners about the injustices being experienced by minority cultures within the parish boundary is truly Christian. However, the first group's planned response assumes that their own cultural ways of praying are God-determined; therefore, they see no need to give them up in their efforts to foster prayer among members of the minority cultures. They arrogantly assume the superiority of Anglo-Saxon culture and that God certainly belongs to their way of life! Their planned pastoral response takes no account of the fact that inculturation may demand they surrender something to which they are deeply attached. In this case, their cultural sense of superiority.

The second group accepts the fact that inculturation involves loss and newness: the loss of a false sense of cultural superiority and an openness to discovering how the Lord can and does work in other cultures. The ritual of mourning, in which forgiveness was asked for their culture's domination over the minority cultures, became a most moving experience of reconciliation.

3. Establishing a Basic Christian Community

A Basic Christian Community—which is sometimes referred to as a Basic Ecclesial Community, House Church, Intentional Christian Community—is a group of individuals or families that know, care for and share with one another, worship together, and seek to center their life, relationships, and activities on Christ.[16]

Pastor George, who is officially in charge of a parish of 100,000 in a Third World nation, felt that his task was an impossible one, since he could not even begin adequately to minister to such a huge number of parishioners. He decided to establish Basic Christian Communities to enable the people to minister to themselves. Having called leaders together, he explained to them the theology of ministries and how people must share and work together. The leaders went away and did what they were told, and after a while many BCCs were established.

From time to time Pastor George would call the leaders to a meeting and tell them what they had to do next. He belonged to a clerical culture that assumed that the lay people must always be told what to do: clergy are the pastoral experts, they have the answers, and the people are there to listen and do what they are told. After a few months, at one of these meetings, one of the leaders objected: 'You ask us here to tell us things. But we have studied the Gospels and now we know that we all have the right to speak, to offer advice and make decisions. You now start listening to us. Stop interfering!' There was wide support for his views at the gathering.

Comment

Pastor George has the theory of collaborative ministry, but is totally unaware of its practical implications. At first the people go along with his clerical authoritarianism, as they have known no other model of Church. However, once they discover through Gospel reflection and prayer the community model of Church, they begin to question their pastor's behavior. They demand their rights. There is an urgent need for Pastor George and for his clerical culture as a whole to allow their authoritarian customs to die; then there would develop an authentic grasp of what collaborative ministry really means.

4. Losing a sacred site

Because of the decline in the number of applicants to a particular province of a religious congregation, their formation house established over a hundred years ago had to be closed. Members of the province had different feelings about the house: some, because they had bitter memories of their formation experiences, were happy to see the house closed as quickly as possible; others retained very positive memories and were sad that the house had to shut down as a formation center.

The provincial (the head of the province) decided that just before the house was to be adapted to a totally new apostolic venture, she would invite members of the province to a liturgy of farewell on site, to be followed by a dinner in the house's old refectory. In the liturgy ample space was provided for people to express in a non-threatening atmosphere their feelings about the house and what it had meant to them. People recounted sad and happy stories about their own involvement in the house's history, and these brought a mixture of tears and laughter.

Comment

Here we have a positive experience of inculturation. The provincial and her team not only had recognized the need for a new apostolic project, they also had sought advice on how to close a house that had ceased to be apostolically relevant, and to reopen it for the new pastoral thrust. They appreciated the need for people to be fully involved in allowing one organizational culture to die, if the new one is to be widely supported. Hence, the decision to invite people to a ritual of mourning resulted in a positive apostolic experience.

At the ritual the provincial formally thanked God for the blessings bestowed on the province over the years through the work of the house; she also asked forgiveness of God for the mistakes committed over the years by the community. She spoke of the physical changes that must now be made to the house to accommodate the new apostolate, and she asked the group to pray with her for God's blessings on this creative venture. She invited participants to feel free to return to the house at any time. At the ritual's end she formally unveiled the new apostolate's title attached to the wall at the entrance to the house. She also recommended, in order to symbolize links with the past, that formators choose some historical items from the building and transfer them to the new and smaller formation house.

5. Opting for and *with* the poor

Ms Smith is a full-time pastoral worker in a parish containing people ranging from extreme wealth to desperate poverty. She had become a tireless worker for the rights of the poor, raising money for their needs, challenging city hall to provide better housing and family relief funds for them. Daily she would leave her home in a middle-class suburb to visit the poor areas, encouraging the people in their efforts to establish political pressure groups. One day an unemployed father of four challenged her: 'We are grateful for your concern for us. Yet, if you truly want to help us and be identified with our cause, why do you still live in affluence? Why don't you live with us? Then we and the rich will believe that you do sincerely want our lives to change!' Ms Smith accepted the challenge and she came to live among the poor.

Comment

The phrase 'option for the poor' is rightly popular today as an inculturation imperative. However, while most may feel this means only that they should work *for* the poor, the group that criticized Ms Smith believed that this was an insufficient commitment. In their view they wanted people willing to identify with their sufferings, for only then would pastoral workers like Ms Smith have credibility with them. Ms Smith accepted the challenge; she felt their complaint was justified, because as long as she remained in the middle-class environment she maintained a security that the poor never possessed.

6. Middle-class Christian practice

The people of St Edwina's parish have just finished the building of a new rectory and parish church. The pastor and his building committee, immensely proud of the new complex, had planned the church in great detail as they wanted the people to worship in a church perfectly designed for the renewal of the liturgy.

Since on the day of the opening it was noticed that only the wealthy and middle-class parishioners participated, the local pastor became anxious to find out why his parishioners from several minority cultures were not present. They had promised him they would be. He asked representatives of the minority groups to visit him and explain why they had not come, but no one turned up. Angry at this, he went to their houses, but no one would respond satisfactorily to his questions, until a spokesman finally and with considerable feeling told him their problems with the new church complex:

> We cannot worship in the church. It is too neat and tidy. We feel ill-at-ease in the church with all those other people so well dressed. We are so anxious that we cannot pray. But worse still. You have thrown out all our favorite saints. You say worship must be simple, just Christ, no saints—but that style is for you professional people. Come with me. See, we were able to save some of those statues from destruction and look, we pray here. Why did you not ask us how we felt about the plans before you built the church?

Comment

Through *popular religiosity* people express their relationships to the deity and the supernatural through very concrete symbols, such as statues, fiestas, rosaries; feeling or imagination is dominant, not rationality or intellectual analysis. People recognize the need for a wide variety of mediators—for example, saints—as agents to intercede for them in a world that is seen to be always working against them.

People with this form of piety are commonly assumed, particularly by middle-class Christians, to have a rather inferior type of relationship with God. Critics assert that concrete symbols of their beliefs are really not important for the nurturing and the expression of one's relationship to God; some even claim that the symbols hinder or obstruct true worship of the Lord.

The planners of the church in St Edwina's parish possess these arrogant theological and cultural assumptions about popular religiosity. If they had understood inculturation they would have involved all sections of the parish in the planning of the church, including people devoted to popular religiosity. This would have meant putting aside their own prejudices about minority cultures, listening to people whose way of life and method of praying are different from their own. They would have understood that the spirituality of inculturation must involve for them as planners a ritual of mourning, that is, the giving up of narrow cultural assumptions about the practice of religion. In return they would have been enriched by the experience of how warm and vital liturgical celebrations can be for people who use their imaginations in its service.[17]

7. Understanding the refounding of Gospel communities

A province of an apostolic religious congregation had at an assembly of its members discussed at considerable length the charism of the foundress. Participants were so genuinely impressed with the founding vision and its relevance for today's world, that they enthusiastically agreed to revitalize their lives according to this vision. The vast majority voted in favor of the following resolution: 'We commit ourselves to a renewal of prayer and community life; we believe that if we pray harder, then we will be refounding the congregation according to the vision of our beloved foundress. We see the need to be careful of the world's temptations.'

Several participants expressed concern about this statement: 'We fully favor any movement that could lead to the revitalization of our prayer life. But the process of refounding is far more than prayer. Surely we must pray harder. But there must also be good works', they said. However, this small group was rejected 'as dangerous leftists who fail to understand what is at the heart of religious life'.

Comment
Refounding a religious congregation, as will be explained more fully in the next chapter, means far more than a renewed commitment to prayer, vitally important though this be. It connotes the pastorally creative response to the evangelization of cultures in the contemporary world.[18] The challenge is just so immense that we must speak of radically new pastoral strategies, because the pastoral methods once suitable to the evangelizing thrust of a ghetto-maintaining Christianity are simply inadequate to confront today's world of secularism, materialism and indifferentism.

The religious in the above case study who recognize this fact are marginalized by other members of the congregation, while the latter have opted for a new form of Christian fundamentalism; that is, a withdrawal from a world that is considered evil or dangerous. The call for Christians to be involved in the struggle for social justice is an integral dimension of inculturation or the mission of the Church; to live the incarnation means being totally committed to evangelize the world of cultures, not to flee from them.

8. Evangelizing youth culture

The pastoral team of St Luke's Anglican parish was so deeply worried about their failure to contact young people that they decided to make two major efforts at evangelization. First, they organized a service explicitly advertised for youth; two team members were excellent teachers, so they arranged for hymns and prayers they believed young people would appreciate. Second, they arranged for a social for youth in the local parish hall. Both programs failed.

At the same time in the next parish the team there planned nothing except to spend the next six months visiting places where youth congregated. At great inconvenience to themselves, team members just listened to what bothered young people who talked with them: unemployment or the fear of it, relationships with one another and with their parents' generation, boredom, pressure to take drugs, peer-group constraints.

Several young people, after watching the team members for five months, were impressed by their patience and their listening gifts, so they offered to work with them for a few months to plan practical responses to these problems. One of these volunteers commented: 'You know, you are not like other adults. You come here, put up with our noise, listen to our anger, do not judge us. We feel you really want to know us. We trust you.' Eventually, an experimental youth center was established well away from the parish complex, where young people could drop in for such services as recreational games and counseling. It is now a popular gathering place for youth, and several on their own initiative are organizing a weekly prayer session for those who wish to participate.

Comment

The major reason for the collapse of the first team's efforts is simple: members failed to understand that the world of youth is *not* a culture of children. They rather arrogantly assumed it was and what youth most needed was 'a good dose of organization from on high'! They never believed they had anything to learn from young people or their culture.

The second team was prepared to die for periods of time to

their own cultural security and assumptions. They recognized that inculturation demands a spirituality of empathetic listening modelled on the approach of Jesus himself in his pastoral ministry. Their approach succeeded.

9. A study in congregational denial

A small international clerical religious congregation established over thirty years ago several houses (which form a 'district') in a country where Christians comprise barely 1 per cent of the population. The potential for conversion is minimal. Efforts have been made in the past to recruit local vocations to the congregation, but with no lasting success.

It was decided a few years ago by the congregational central administration, after an in-depth analysis and discussions with the men in the district, to cease all efforts at local recruitment. In a lengthy report to the district, the central government concluded that further efforts to recruit locally would be unjust to candidates, *if* perchance any did apply.

The major reasons given for this decision were:

—the possibility of obtaining vocations is very slight indeed, because of the smallness of the Christian community and the presence of several other clerical religious congregations committed to recruiting.
—as the average age of the district's membership is 63, it is almost certain that the district must close within ten to fifteen years and any local recruits would then have to transfer to another country.
—community life is almost non-existent, as the district's members live alone and in houses that would be impossible to maintain without foreign aid; recruits could not reasonably expect, therefore, the support of a community according to the charism of the congregation, even in their training period.
—the district is staffed predominantly by volunteers from the United States and their monocultural background has negative pastoral consequences: when members assemble, conversations are in English and generally revolve around the latest ball game or political event in North America; former local recruits to the district found this 'little America' emphasis embarrassing and hurtful.
—the methods of evangelization had not, with some

exceptions, changed over the years; authoritarian clericalism, together with an uncritical acceptance of pre-Vatican II American pastoral methods, gave little hope that change could ever take place; in this atmosphere local recruits would find it difficult, if not impossible, to develop pastoral methods based on the principles of inculturation.

It was recommended to the district that it focus all its energies on the development of the laity within the local Church. The congregation could then at the right time be able to withdraw after establishing a highly committed group of lay people to take over the role of evangelization. Every effort should also be made to foster priestly vocations to the local diocese, because it had only a very small number of local priests.

The decision, with its accompanying explanations, was immediately and *vigorously* rejected by the majority in the district. Comments like the following were made:

'We have every right to recruit people for religious life. That is our task and the local Church should look after its own problems and challenges. Our task here is to keep going.'

'The person who put this report together knows nothing whatsoever about this country. We are the experts, for we have been here for years!'

'We need locals to take over our work, just as it is. There is no need to change. Our pastoral methods worked in the past and they do so now.'

'There are some in our district who are doing new things. They must stop this and rejoin us to do the ordinary nitty gritty pastoral projects, for that is where the priest fulfills his vocation.'

'Recruits must accept us as we are; we will teach them to pray and be obedient.'

'The central administration is against us. They are stopping volunteers coming to this district.'

'Look at all we have done to develop our pastoral centers! Local people should be grateful for what we have done for them. Local recruits would have an easy time taking over from us; all is prepared for them.'

'We do have a fine community life, even though we do not live together. Look how we enjoy ourselves when we come together monthly!'

Comment

The above personal reactions are symptoms that the district's culture is experiencing grief. The identity of the culture is severely threatened and it wants to survive at all costs, even if this means that the local diocese and people must suffer.

Reflect on some of the signs of anger and chronic denial. Members should recognize the fact, but refuse to do so, that it is impossible to obtain volunteers from elsewhere in the congregation, and for many years no local person has asked to join the congregation. The congregational central administration is seen as the scapegoat for the district's troubles. The district has failed to foster a process of inculturation; they refuse to see that they are attempting to implant in the country an American way of life and pastoral action.

There is the failure to see that no local recruit could survive as long as the district's culture remains unchanged, because any pastoral creative talent he might possess would be suffocated by its pastoral and cultural ethnocentric pressures. The small minority within the district who have positively grieved over the situation is trying to foster inculturation, but the majority of members are out to domesticate them back to the traditional ways of doing things. In the meantime, members of the minority are considered 'traitors to the district' and continue to grieve over the pastoral blindness and cultural insensitivities of the majority.

This case study demonstrates the truth of this book's thesis: the letting go of the familiar and secure past and present is the severest test of nerve and vision, for institutions as much as for individuals. In this instance, a district congregational culture has developed over years which has become locked-in on chronic denial. Corporate denial, in other words, had become an accepted way of life long before the report of the central administration reached the district. The report merely made the denial and anger over the grief more vociferous. If the district had entered a grieving process a long time ago, then it would not have become and remained a 'little America' of a pre-Vatican II pastoral mold transplanted in a highly sophisticated foreign culture.

The central congregational leadership acted correctly in presenting the report to the district, but the same type of challenging should have been done by successive administrations years before. Unjust pastoral structures had been allowed to emerge unchecked, because previous administrations had failed to see that one of their most critically important roles is to call congregational members to a process of personal and corporate grieving. Because this had not been done, the local Church had pastorally suffered and formation methods for local recruits (since left) had been fostered that were culturally and humanly offensive, if not unjust.

Summary

The theologian John A. Robinson writes that 'The traditional . . . way of describing the Incarnation almost invariably suggests that Jesus was really God almighty walking about the earth, dressed up as a man'.[19] This view is totally false, for it denies the incredible mystery whereby Jesus enters through the incarnation into a loving exchange: God is drawn into humankind and humankind enters into the Godhead. God becomes weary, laughs, suffers, grieves, weeps, dies.

When we preach the Gospel of Christ, we also must expect this same exchange process to take place: the giving up of ourselves and all that would interfere with the proclamation of his message and the dramatic discovery in return of seeing the Spirit active in the lives of people, so often different from our own. A spirituality that is not vigorously rooted in the mystery of the incarnation cannot long sustain us as partners with Christ in his mission to the world.

Discussion questions

1. Is there any statement about evangelization in this chapter that members of the group disagree with? Why?

2. Why does the preaching and receiving of the Good News require us to undergo personal and cultural grieving rituals?

3. What case study in this chapter particularly appeals to the group? Why? Could members of the group give their own case studies to illustrate the theory of the chapter?

References

1. For a more detailed analysis, see G. A. Arbuckle, *Earthing the Gospel: An Inculturation Handbook for Pastoral Workers* (London: Geoffrey Chapman; Maryknoll, NY: Orbis Books, 1990), *passim*; also L. J. Luzbetak, *The Church and Cultures: New Perspectives in Missiological Anthropology* (Maryknoll, NY: Orbis Books, 1988), pp. 64–105; A. Shorter, *Toward a Theology of Inculturation* (London: Geoffrey Chapman, 1988), *passim*.

2. M. de C. Azevedo, *Inculturation and the Challenge of Modernity* (Rome: Gregorian University, 1982), p. 11.

3. See Paul VI, *Evangelii Nuntiandi*, 1975, para. 20; for a somewhat similar ecumenical view, see 'Mission and evangelism: an ecumenical affirmation', *International Review of Mission*, vol. 71, no. 284 (1982), p. 438.

4. See 'Pastoral Constitution on the Church in the Modern World', para. 44.

5. See Paul VI, *Evangelii Nuntiandi*, op. cit., para. 63.

6. 'The Gospel According to John' in R. Brown *et al.* (eds), *The Jerome Biblical Commentary* (London: Geoffrey Chapman, 1968), p. 423.

7. See R. Brown, *The Gospel According to John I–XII* (New York: Doubleday, 1966), pp. 30–5.

8. See D. Patte, *The Gospel According to Matthew: A Structural Commentary on Matthew's Faith* (Philadelphia: Fortress Press, 1987), pp. 185–92.

9. See A. Weiser, *The Psalms: A Commentary* (London: SCM Press, 1962), pp. 760–3.

10. See H. Conzelmann, *Acts of the Apostles* (Philadelphia: Fortress Press, 1987), pp. 115–21, and M. Hengel, *Acts and the History of Earliest Christianity* (London: SCM Press, 1987), pp. 111–26.

11. See J. Fitzmyer, *The Gospel According to Luke I–IX* (New York: Doubleday, 1981), pp. 792–7.

12. R. F. O'Toole, 'Luke's message in Luke 9:1–50', *The Catholic Biblical Quarterly*, vol. 49, no. 1 (1987), p. 77.

13. See I. H. Marshall, *The Gospel of Luke* (Exeter: Paternoster Press, 1978), pp. 403–8.

14. *Dictionary of the Bible* (London: Geoffrey Chapman, 1965), p. 766.

15. See G. A. Arbuckle, *Strategies for Growth in Religious Life* (New York: Alba House, 1987), pp. 203–35.

16. See Arbuckle, *Earthing the Gospel*, op. cit., pp. 86ff.

17. See G. A. Arbuckle, 'Dress and worship: liturgies for the culturally dispossessed', *Worship*, vol. 59, no. 5 (1985), pp. 426–35.

18. See relevant comments by J. W. O'Malley, 'Priesthood, ministry, and religious life: some historical and historiographical considerations', *Theological Studies*, vol. 49 (1988), pp. 223–57.

19. *Honest to God* (Philadelphia: Westminster Press, 1963), pp. 65f.

Chapter 7

CALLING TO MOURN:
LEADERSHIP AND REFOUNDING

> Prophetic ministry consists of offering an alternative perception
> of reality and in letting people see their own history in the light
> of God's freedom and his will for justice. . . . Mourning is a
> precondition. . . . Only that kind of anguished disengagement
> permits fruitful yearning and only the public embrace of death-
> liness permits newness to come (Walter Brueggemann).[1]

The basic theme of this book so far is that healing involves
the readiness and the courage on the part of individuals,
organizations, and cultures to allow the past to die. It also
means arranging space for the new to emerge and be received.
And ritual holds a critically important role in allowing the
healing after loss to occur, and the new to come forth.

Thus, if a Gospel community has unresolved grief, it is
ignoring the chance to heal the inevitable hurts of loss; consequently, it cannot face the pastoral challenges of the contemporary world with the creative freshness and boldness that the
mission of Christ calls it to. Significant loss for a Christian
involves the relationship of human mortality to the mystery of
Christ's resurrection as inseparably as Calvary is related to
Easter. Thus, if the grief of communities or cultures is to be
resolved adequately, mourning rituals are necessary in which
the fact of loss is acknowledged.

In this chapter I describe the qualities of those people who
must be the ritual leaders of grieving for Gospel communities.
Their task is a crucial one. I describe three types of ritual
leaders: refounding persons, creative change agents, and the
officially appointed community leaders. Since the historical role
of Moses as a ritual leader of community mourning is especially
detailed and powerfully effective, we will examine his behavior
to illustrate the ways in which today's administrators of Gospel
communities should act as ritual leaders.

'Refounding' and 'creative' persons as ritual leaders

Back in the 1960s the mainline Churches opened themselves with a fantastic burst of apostolic enthusiasm to a world of change, turning their backs at least in theory on centuries of inward-looking defensive action. The high hopes we had created back there that the world was waiting to listen to us have never been realized.

Since then the tide of change has further intensified: the rich nations are becoming richer, the poor poorer; Eastern Europe is breaking away with lightning speed from the Marxist oppression; countries are being torn apart by bitter age-old racial and ethnic rivalries; a fundamentalist backlash against modernization and the speed of change, sometimes violent, is dividing Islamic peoples, and is even finding a welcome home in many sections of the Christian Churches.

On the other hand, there are many hopeful signs that creation is 'groaning in labour pains . . . to be set free' (Rom 8:22f.) from secular and/or religious oppression. For instance, there is a 'profound sense that the earth is "suffering" '[2] through the sustained misuse of its resources; powerful forces are working towards political unity in parts of the world, such as in Western Europe, where co-operation seemed utterly impossible a few decades ago; women are demanding and beginning to achieve in some cultures their rightful equality and the demise of the patriarchal society.

How are the Churches reacting to these and other momentous changes in the marketplace? Overall, the response is uneven. There is a widespread malaise or feeling of chaos about how to relate the Gospel life to even the positive movements in the world. Many Christians feel that they are only passive observers of events, or that the Churches merely react to crises and fail to anticipate them with imaginative and creative pastoral responses. This should not be, however, too surprising. The predictable world of a ghetto-Church has been a poor training ground for evangelizers to learn how to respond creatively and proactively to such pastoral challenges. Pastoral methods that worked in a static environment simply are inadequate today. The simplistic directives of fundamentalists, who dream of dragging the Churches away from interaction with the world, are no solution at all.

Some local Churches have fostered creative pastoral

programs based on theologies adapted to the poverty around them—for example, liberation theology in South America. Generally, however, in the affluent Western world we often seem powerless to act when faced with secularism, materialism, and de-Christianized societies. Because the pastoral challenges are so immense and complex, I prefer to speak of the need today 'to refound the Church', not institutionally, but strategically. That is, we need new apostolic strategies that can help us relate the Gospel to problems that a few decades ago we knew little or nothing about.

Therefore, when we speak of refounding the Church we mean that it is responding to the type of pastoral need described above. Finally, the process of refounding has nothing *directly* to do with getting at all costs new recruits into the Gospel communities; for example, parishes, religious congregations. Refounding is not the numbers game! In fact, the call to refound can frighten the less committed away, encouraging them to seek refuge in a more comforting and mediocre Gospel lifestyle. Refounding is a process whereby people bind together to live a more authentic Gospel life and struggle to respond to the most urgent, non-ephemeral needs of today; others may or may not be drawn to follow them.

CASE STUDIES

The following case study helps to illustrate the nature of what is meant by the contemporary refounding of Gospel life. Notice how some people became fearful of the Gospel challenge because they did not want to lose their secure lifestyle, if they committed themselves to struggle for justice in their own nation. So they moved away from the young Gospel community.

> In a Manila parish, in the Philippines, a well-to-do businessman, Arturo, reflected on the apostolic sterility of his local parish, so he talked this over with some of his wealthy friends. They were initially enthusiastic. While leading his companions through a discussion on the Gospel beatitudes, he suddenly realized that the poor had not been invited to join them. He explained this to his friends, but they responded with all kinds of excuses when he next invited them to pray with him about the social justice demands of the Gospel. They were frightened that a better knowledge of the Gospel would require that they alter their rich lifestyles and unite with the poor in the struggle for social justice. This they could not

take, so they gradually withdrew from the Gospel discussion group. They were prepared to 'hand out charity', they said, but never to become involved in any fight for social justice.

Arturo then turned to his poor neighbors and over time formed a Basic Christian Community with them. The more he became part of the lives of the poor, the more he could see that the battle to liberate people from economic and political poverty was at the heart of the message of Christ. But, he said, he had first to liberate himself from attachments to security symbols: his excessive wealth, prayer centered primarily on himself and not on the needs around him.

Arturo's lifestyle became simpler. 'The more I worked with the poor, the more', he said, 'I found my prayer drawing me closer to Christ the Liberator.' He began to pray, he said, with a deeper conviction as he became increasingly involved with the poor and further marginalized by his rich friends. Arturo now daily risks his life as he battles against corruption in high places and as he petitions for the rights of the poor. 'I look back on the last few years. I see what I gave up in worldly terms, but I also see the exciting newness of my life in Christ and in the lives of the powerless.'

Elsewhere I have argued at length[3] that we now need people, like Arturo in the above case study, with creative imaginations and deep faith commitment, who devise and implement methods of evangelization suited to a radically different world from their fathers and mothers. More precisely, I define the apostolic refounding persons as those who:

—in response to the inspiration of the Holy Spirit,
—are deeply disturbed in faith when they perceive the gap between the Gospel and the contemporary world caused through injustices, materialism, secularism, indifferentism to the Gospel message,
—and are able to devise and *implement* imaginative and creative ways to help bridge this gap;
—and at the same time, they restlessly summon others to faith/justice conversion and to share in the Gospel vision to risk going out into the unknown world, in order to implement the pastoral strategies.

The definition assumes a basic fact of experience that ultimately certain individuals have particular gifts of imagination, creativity, and drive to the level required for refounding. They have that gift of offering the world 'an alternative perception of reality and [of] letting people see their own history in the light of God's freedom and his will for justice'.[4] They have the ability to break through the present-day barriers to Gospel life: injustice/the oppression of the poor, secularism, materialism.

Others do not possess this gift. And this can be an uncomfortable truth, to discover that some people have gifts I do not have, especially of leadership. This truth causes tension within the young churches in St Paul's time; people do not want to face the truth that others have natural and supernatural gifts they do not possess. So Paul vigorously reiterates the truth that the Spirit gives 'gifts to humanity . . . to some, his "gift" was that they should be apostles; to some prophets; to some, evangelists; to some, pastors and teachers; to knit God's holy people together for the work of service to build up the Body of Christ' (Eph 4:8, 11f.).

The gift of refounding Gospel communities comes from the Holy Spirit and it is a gift of prophecy, a talent especially esteemed by St Paul (1 Cor 14:1). We cannot give this grace to ourselves nor to others. Those who possess this gift are uncompromising in their proclamation of the full message of the Lord; Yahweh's words to Jeremiah energize Gospel community refounding persons: 'let anyone who wants to boast, boast of this: of understanding and knowing me. For I am Yahweh, who acts with faithful love, justice, and uprightness on earth; yes, these are what please me' (9:23f.). Like all prophets, however, refounding persons generally suffer for their efforts; people feel their comfortable security is threatened by the radical apostolic insights, or they simply cannot grasp what the prophets are saying.

Planning committees and supportive structures may be helpful, even necessary, in fostering and supporting the development of the prophetic gifts of the apostolic creative individuals referred to by St Paul. However, the filing cabinets of many religious congregations, diocesan archives and parishes are filled with brilliant plans devised in countless meetings; they gather dust as long as there are no individuals with the imagination and courage to implement these apostolic blueprints. Action occurs only when individuals of prophetic qualities, supported by the right structures and communities, have the space to act.

Refounding persons are impelled by the love of the Lord to

act, and those who feel drawn by the Gospel vision of these imaginative persons come to recognize their own need to turn to the Lord with converting hearts. Without this underlying conversion there can be no refounding. If people are authentically refounding persons, they have those qualities of the Spirit that St Paul refers to: 'love, joy, peace, patience, kindness, goodness, trustfulness, gentleness and self-control. . . . All who belong to Christ Jesus have crucified self with all its passions and its desires' (Gal 5:22–24). Because they have these qualities, refounding persons recognize the need to seek the advice and insights of others in a collaborative way; for them, the building of a community of faith sharing and action is an indispensable way to build a Gospel community. Authentic refounding persons are definitely not loners or little dictators! They are community people, because they yearn to share their Gospel vision with others and build communities of sharing, faith, love, and hope.

Observe finally the phrase in the definition: refounding persons are 'deeply disturbed'. They grieve, as do Jeremiah and Jesus, when they see how people are deprived of the knowledge of God's love for them and are enslaved by the structures of sin or injustice. They strive to invite people to disengage themselves from this world of death to permit Gospel newness to emerge.[5] Refounding persons are ritual mourners *par excellence*.

I refer above to the second category of people: 'creative persons'. Prophets of the type we need to face the contemporary challenges are rather rare in history; creative pastoral persons are to be found more commonly among us. Though they lack the gifts of refounding persons, they feel drawn to follow the Gospel community vision of refounding people. They bring their talents into a collaborative ministry with the latter, or they help to foster a climate within the Churches that is open to receive the prophetic people, if and when the Spirit offers them to us. Creative pastoral persons are of all kinds. For example, they may be *oppression interpreters*; that is, they are people who help the oppressed understand the causes of their enslavement; they may be *encouragers* of those who feel fearful to struggle for justice or who wrongly believe that they have no potential for self-growth; they may be *compassionate agents* of Christ's healing for those overwhelmed by their own sense of sin and shame.

The following are several case studies that may help readers to understand the above theory:

1. Reorienting an elite college

A religious congregation had been directing a college for the sons and daughters of rich families for over a hundred years. In recent years several teachers became aware for the first time that the congregation had been originally established to educate the very poor and socially marginalized, but they felt powerless to do anything about it.

However, Father X, deeply committed to Gospel justice and the original charism of the congregation, devised a plan to reorientate the college in favor of the poor. For several years he failed to win acceptance from his congregation for his plan. Comments such as the following were directed at him: 'The rich have souls also, you know! . . . Times have changed since the founder's day. . . . His insights must be updated. . . . We would be more impressed if you spent more time with the pupils we have than in running night classes for those lazy migrant peoples down the road.' Father X did not become bitter or cynical, but kept hoping that some people would see the relevance of his vision.

Finally, the small group of teachers concerned for the poor grew a little larger, and one of their number was chosen as the college's rector. Negotiations developed with the marginalized Father X and he was brought in to explain his integrated vision of a college refounded on the principles of the authentic congregational charism. Under his direction, a team developed a program of compensatory education for the poor and the successful pupils were admitted into the school. Religion classes were reoriented to explain what is meant by the faith/justice mission of Jesus, and volunteers from the rich pupils became involved in helping with the compensatory education program for the poor. A significant number of parents objected to the 'dangerous socialist' vision of the school, and withdrew their sons and daughters.

2. Refounding Church in an affluent society

Some members of a college alumni association at the annual dinner began discussing the problems they were having in their parish churches; for example, the poor quality of the sermons and liturgical services, the lack of community support for families, and solid Gospel instruction for young people. As discussions continued, some expressed dissatisfaction with their own alumni association; it seemed to be concerned only with planning annual dinners committed, as one critic said, 'to drinking and the repeating of stories of an adolescent past'.

A few months later one member of the group wrote back to others who had been involved in the discussion and proposed the beginnings of a solution: 'If we can come together once a year for a meal, why not meet again to pray about our parish problems?' Several agreed and the meeting was held. As a result, there emerged three pastoral support groups in different geographical areas, organizing prayer sessions for themselves and Gospel instruction classes for their families. After a few months they recognized the need to share their faith with others, so they planned various outreach programs. Five years later, there are ten such groups spread over a wide area of the diocese. Most groups are flourishing, but the local parish leaders commonly consider them to be 'dangerous and elitist', because of their emphasis on prayer sessions and their concern for faith/justice programs for the poor.

3. Building a Basic Christian Community

Boy, with five children, was a cane-cutter on a large sugar estate in the Philippines. The owners of the estate have been ruthlessly oppressing the cane-cutters for over a hundred years, giving them a pittance for their work. Boy became increasingly angry with the oppressive conditions, and one day invited some fellow workers to his poverty-stricken hut to pray about their common problems.

He started by reciting the text: 'Blessed are those who hunger and thirst for uprightness: they shall have their fill' (Mt 5:6). He realized then he must struggle for the rights of the cane-cutters and asked his companions to join him. Most did, and they approached the estate's manager to ask for an increase in their wages, but they were rudely ignored. The following day a piece of paper was found on the floor of Boy's hut: 'Stop this talk of higher wages. If not, we kill you!' Boy did not stop and he and the group prayed for strength to keep up their campaign for justice, but a few days later a jeep sped past Boy's hut and sprayed it with bullets, killing Boy and two of his children. People are too frightened to identify their killers.

4. The socially concerned executive

An executive, Alice, of a large North American company began to feel the pressures of her work to be almost overwhelming. She needed space and spiritual nourishment, so one day she pinned a note to a board in the executive dining room inviting people to a breakfast prayer session. Six came, and for several months she and others appreciated the chance to pause from the pressures of work and pray together about their worries with the aid of appropriate texts from the Scriptures.

Alice began to sense, however, that real issues of life were not being faced in the ecumenical prayer sessions; people were too turned in on themselves and on their own personal needs. She suggested to the group that it might consider the morality of the firm's operations: for example, as the raw materials are from Africa, are the suppliers being paid justly? Are executives being expected to give up their family life in order to maintain their jobs? If so, what should they do about it? Is the profit motive far too strong in the company to the detriment of other human values?

When the firm's top executives, not part of the prayer group, heard of the new social justice orientation they became angry; up to that point they thought the group's prayer emphasis was excellent as it made the participants more content as workers. Crises developed when the excessive capitalistic values of the company began to be questioned at executive meetings; Alice and the group refused to cease questioning.

Eventually the members of the prayer/study/action group were forced out of the firm. After difficult times, Alice managed to find jobs for herself and others in another firm, but with dramatically reduced salaries. The group continues its activities in more congenial surroundings and Alice is now helping a second group in another firm to be established along the same lines.

5. Fostering hope for the dispossessed

I worked briefly with Frank, who had given his life to the pastoral care of an ethnic group living as a dispossessed people in a country that had once been their own. He would rise early to pray for an hour and a half and then be on the road to visit families and individuals over a wide area. Sometimes he would stop and ring those he felt he could not reach that day, but who were in particular need of pastoral assistance.

After studying his methods I discovered that he had developed a then quite unique way of relating to dispossessed people. Having shrewdly understood that decades of oppression had undermined their culture and therefore their sense of personal and group self-worth, he recognized that his major work had to be on a one-to-one level. He would spend his time repeatedly trying to encourage individuals to discover that they had personal gifts that needed to be developed. One person told me:

> When he comes to visit, we all feel so much better. He has the gift of helping us to be proud of who we are. He helped us to own up to our sufferings and be open to the rediscovery of our dignity as a people. This was a tough job because we disappointed ourselves and him over and over again. But he would come back and try again—not judging us, but believing in us. I am a school teacher because of him. Many times I would have stopped studying because I became so discouraged, but he would ring me or visit me and tell me I could do it. Now, I do the same for others, just like he did to me.

One day we visited a house of his religious congregation after a particularly demanding few hours relating to social problems. During his stay his confrères, without realizing what they were doing, spent the time joking at his expense. No one ever asked him what he had been doing that day. Afterwards, I asked him why he still keeps visiting his congregational communities for the pattern of reception is the same everywhere: 'I go because they are my brothers. They do not understand, but I must love them in Christ.' No bitterness—only charity.

In the light of the theory, the case studies are self-explanatory. However, notice in each case that there is a sincere effort by people I would consider to be refounding persons to build Gospel communities with the collaborative assistance of pastorally creative people, but with varying degrees of success. The last case study illustrates qualities that St Paul said should mark the prophet, that is, prayerfulness, love, patience in rejection. At the heart of each case study there is the same call by the leaders to draw others or groups into a process of Christian grieving. That is, these refounding persons are calling people to discover the fullness of the Gospel message. This first means discarding whatever does not conform to this Good News. It means taking a risk in faith, love, and hope.

Official leaders as ritual leaders

By 'official leaders' I refer to those people who have been formally appointed to administrative leadership positions. Their task is the day-to-day running of the organization or Gospel community. Generally they are selected because they can be trusted to keep the organization ticking over. The tendency, as organizations become well established, is for administrators to become overly concerned with reactive decision-making; that is, they administer mainly by reacting to crises or needs as they emerge. They hesitate to anticipate crises or develop forward-looking policies on the basis of frequently evaluated goals and objectives. Such an approach, if left unchecked, is the death sentence for any organization.

What then should administrators do to foster the refounding of Gospel communities? I will summarize briefly what I have written elsewhere and add refinements in line with the theme of this book:[6]

A. In the short term

1. Discover who, if any, are potentially refounding and/or the pastorally creative persons under their administration.
2. Place them in positions within the community where their creative potential will be best realized.
3. Provide them with structural independence and clear lines of accountability to protect them from outside interference; in this way their energies will not be dissipated in defending themselves and their work.

B. In the long term

1. Foster a collaborative ministry atmosphere, in which people are united through discipleship and ministry into a community that exists for ongoing creative evangelization.[7]
2. Recognize the symptoms of grieving—for example, denial—and develop appropriate mourning strategies.
3. Any ritual, for example, of celebration or mourning, conducted by the community leader must highlight the fact that conversion calls us to let go of apostolically irrelevant attitudes and customs and to be open to any new effective way of preaching the Good News.

4. Since ritual is potentially a most powerful form of communi-
cation, the community leader must spend sufficient time to
prepare it, with the help of knowledgeable people and those
who are to participate in it; a sloppy ritual of mourning, in
which the necessary threefold stages referred to in Chapters
2, 4 and 5 are ill-developed, loudly conveys to people that
apostolic newness is not important.

Moses: an exemplar of the administrative ritual leader

Administrators may be heartened to reflect on the life of one
of the greatest and most successful organizational administrators in history. He is an exemplary administrator because
he is able to lead his community through an extremely difficult
rite of passage; from a motley tribe they become through a
wilderness experience of grieving a people with a known destiny. Moses is aware that there is a distinction between individuals and their community/culture; hence, if people are to
be open to the new, there must be rites of passage for individuals *and* the community/culture (see Figure 4.2 on p. 83).

In the time of Joseph the Jewish people live peacefully in
Egypt, enjoying at the same time considerable political power.
Things change dramatically under Pharaoh, for 'the Israelites
are now more numerous and stronger' (Ex 1:9), so the Israelites
become an oppressed people, with all kinds of heavy work
being 'imposed on them without mercy' (Ex 1:14).

However, Pharaoh recognizes that the Israelites over a long
period are not producing as much as he wants them to, so he
intensifies the oppression. Then he begins to learn the hard
lesson: the old ways of forcing the Israelites to work are no
longer as successful as they used to be, no matter how much
pressure he places on them. But Pharaoh hesitates to change
his ways. The coming of the ten plagues finally shakes Pharaoh
into realizing that the old oppressive approach to the Israelites
will no longer be effective. It would be better to let them leave
the country with haste: 'The Egyptians urged the people on
and hurried them out of the country because, they said,
"Otherwise we shall all be dead" ' (Ex 12:33).

Moses, the wise leader, protects his own people from the
plagues by doing what Yahweh tells him; he makes sure that
blood is sprinkled on the door-posts and the lintels of the

houses: 'When I see the blood I shall pass over you, and you will escape the destructive plague when I strike Egypt' (12:13). He recognizes, as all good administrators should today, that if a new community is to emerge the good elements of the past must be carried over, to allow the new to be built on sound foundations. Thus, Moses, acting on the instructions of Yahweh, identifies through the sprinkling of the blood the pivotal people who have to be protected that they may later become the nucleus of Yahweh's new nation. They are not to be swallowed up in the chaos in which the old is destroyed.

Administrators must be able to recognize the symptoms of grieving and take appropriate ritual action, for Moses did precisely that. He recognizes that in the *separation* stage of the ritual of mourning people feel the pain of leaving the old and familiar world behind; there is hurting, anger, the move to blame others for their misery: 'To Moses they said: "Was it for lack of graves in Egypt, that you had to lead us out to die in the desert? What was the point of bringing us out of Egypt. . . . We prefer to work for the Egyptians than to die in the desert . . ." (Ex 14:11f.). "Why did we not die at Yahweh's hand in Egypt, where we used to sit round the flesh pots and could eat to our heart's content!" ' (Ex 16:3).

Moses (with Yahweh) acts in four ways to turn the grieving into a positive liminal experience to allow the new to emerge. First, he shrewdly understands the importance of permitting the people to experience the chaos. The new cannot develop without pain:

> Remember the long road by which Yahweh your God led you for forty years in the desert, to humble you, to test you and know your inmost heart—whether you would keep his commandments or not. He humbled you, he made you feel hunger. . . . Learn from this that Yahweh your God was training you as a man trains his child . . . (Dt 8:2, 3, 5).

Secondly, he is thoroughly conscious of his own limitations as a leader, so he constantly pleads with Yahweh to help him.[8] Yahweh responds to the prayers of Moses by turning back the Red Sea that allows the Israelites through, but destroys the pursuing Egyptians. The destruction of the oppressors dramatically witnesses to the passing of the old and the consequent feeling that the new is already with the Israelites.

Thirdly, Moses appreciates the need in the *liminal* period of wandering in the desert to keep ties with the collective roots of his people back in Egypt. Hence, he collects the bones of Joseph and allows the people to carry them into the wilderness (Ex 13:19).

Fourthly, at certain points, to mark progress in the journey through the wilderness chaos, Moses appreciates the need for rituals that encourage people to continue to let go of the past's negative aspects and to express hope in the future. Thus, there are the rituals of the sweet water (Ex 15:25), the manna and quails (Ex 16), the water from the rock (Ex 17:1–7). He believes that rituals must be well prepared and speak not just to the mind of participants, but also to their feelings, so he becomes a master of the use of liturgical songs and visual aids.

Moses is aware throughout the exodus journey that the disintegration or the experience of chaos required for a new people to develop can, if not guided prudently, lead to total destruction. Therefore, he sought advice and Jethro, his father-in-law, said, 'Now listen to the advice I am going to give you . . .' (Ex 18:19), and he instructs Moses to group the people into manageable administrative units under the direction of 'capable and God-fearing men, men who are trustworthy and incorruptible' (Ex 18:21). Moses is bluntly reminded that he needs space to think and pray in order to discover the overall vision and plans required to lead the people into a new land (Ex 18:19f.). He heeds the advice.

Released from the burdensome details of maintenance management, Moses now has time to listen to Yahweh and communicate Yahweh's plan and strategies (the Ten Commandments) for the emergence of a new people. By timely references to the vision and the commandments, Moses is able to remind the people of the new world to come once the purifying wilderness experience is ended. Thus the people are held together and the forces of chaos do not get out of control:

> But Yahweh your God is bringing you into a fine country, a land of streams and springs, of waters that well up from the deep in valleys and hills, a land of wheat and barley. . . . Be careful not to forget Yahweh . . . by neglecting his commandments, customs and laws which I am laying down for you today (Dt 8:7, 8, 11).

The lessons that Moses leaves every administrative head of a Gospel community are:

1. Be good listeners. Moses is open to hear Yahweh and to

be aware of the people's sufferings; he keeps contact with the people by wandering around the camps listening and speaking informally to people outside their tents.

2. Recognize that communities/cultures/organizations can suffer grief and show all its symptoms. Their experience of grief can be creative, if rituals of mourning are encouraged. As Brueggemann says: 'The public sharing of pain is one way to let the reality sink in and let death go'.[9]

3. If grieving is to be a positive experience for a community, then the administrator, personally or through others, must construct rituals of mourning, according to a definite structure and process; the administrator should never delegate the leadership role in particularly important community rituals of mourning—for example, the closing of an important house or apostolate of the community.

4. Understand that the liminal experience of chaos/wilderness is crucial, if people are to let go of the old and be open to the new. Moses had tremendous courage to allow the chaos to continue; he resists the powerful temptation to jump in and stop people from experiencing the disintegration of their sense of identity and belonging derived from their sojourn in Egypt.

Remember that we Westerners are culturally resistant to any experience of significant loss or chaos; we expect change to happen painlessly and speedily. Hence, we need repeatedly to ponder the lessons of the wilderness for the Israelites. The forty years that they spend in the desert is a metaphorical way of saying that it takes a very long time for a new cultural identity to develop. In fact, an entirely new generation emerges with no firsthand knowledge of Egypt as a source of identity. In the desert chaos they become bonded together and begin to interiorize over a lengthy period the new vision that Moses conveys to them. Thus the Israelites who finally leave the wilderness are a radically different people from the generation that had fled Egypt.

5. Realize that chaos must not be allowed to lead to total disintegration; people throughout the liminal period need a clear and inspiring vision of what they should be aiming at, as well as the structures and rituals that help them to maintain unity; these facilitate the process whereby the past can be allowed to slip away and hope in the future fostered.

6. Be comfortable with the chaos in one's own personal journey. Unless one is able to mourn personally for one's own

sins and losses, it will be impossible to be sensitive to the grieving needs of a community. This means the structuring of time and space to be with oneself and with God; feverish busyness is no atmosphere for contemplation, self-knowledge, and creativity.

7. Moses sought the advice of Jethro, the first management consultant. Administrators must not hesitate to seek the advice/ assistance of people skilled in all kinds of group leadership; for example, management consultants, social psychologists, group grief counsellors, cultural and pastoral anthropologists, liturgists.[10]

However, if these specialists are to be employed in facilitating change/mourning within Gospel communities, administrative heads must first spell out clearly beforehand the terms of reference for their involvement. These specialists must be prepared to respect the Christian ethic of these communities and ultimately such people must be accountable to the administrative heads (and advisers) of the communities.

8. Poor Moses, hardworking and zealous in the service of Yahweh and the people, experiences intense loneliness and social marginalization. Even his closest friends bitterly attack him (Nb 12:1), and finally he himself does not reach the promised land. Yet he struggles to remain faithful and we are told how: 'Moses was extremely humble, the humblest man on earth' (Nb 12:3). Whoever is called to lead one's brothers and sisters from chaos to incarnational conversion requires considerable detachment and humility—the virtues that are at the heart of all successful mourning.

Moses was humble because he prayed. A man naturally impatient and with a powerful temper (Ex 2:12; 32:19), Moses could never have survived the trials of leadership without constantly praying to Yahweh from the anguish of his own inner chaos. Moses is often depicted at prayer, begging Yahweh to recognize his own weaknesses and those of the Israelites. There is the touching scene in which 'Moses' arms grew heavy [at prayer], so they took a stone and put it under him and on this he sat, with Aaron and Hur supporting his arms on each side' (Ex 17:11f.). Armed with the self-knowledge of his own inner unworthiness gained through prayer, Moses becomes a deeply compassionate and patient person.

His detachment and humility are eminently evident in his relationship with his successor and in the manner in which he accepts his own death outside the promised land. He promises the people that Joshua will lead them across into the promised land. He does not criticize Joshua for lack of experience, as one less detached would have done, but actually goes out of his way to support Joshua publicly: 'Be strong, stand firm, have no fear, do not be afraid . . . Yahweh your God . . . will not fail you' (Dt 31:6). Then Yahweh called Moses to die alone on a mountain, having merely glimpsed the promised land from its height. Moses accepted his death and the circumstances in which it was to take place with a spirit of remarkable patience and detachment (Dt 34:1–7). Moses, having long practised the art of grieving over his own failings, was able to the end to be the ritual leader *par excellence* of his people in their grieving process.

CASE STUDY: THE RITES OF PASSAGE OF A GOSPEL COMMUNITY

St Martin's is a province of a male religious congregation in North America. At two chapters (administrative planning meetings of elected members) in 1981 and 1985, the reports of the provincial (administrative head of the province) graphically portrayed through statistical analysis the stark realities of the rising average age (65 years) of the province, the failure to recruit new members (none since 1981), and the difficulties in continuing to staff present apostolic commitments.

However, despite efforts by the provincial to have the reports thoroughly debated, chapter delegates very quickly arranged the agenda to avoid little more than a cursory discussion of the reports. Both chapters closed without the delegates ever confronting the matters of the provincial reports. A minority group at the chapters attempted several times to turn debate back to the realities of the reports, but on each occasion other chapter delegates skillfully directed discussion to less-threatening topics. The chapters ended with statements assuring the province that it was in good shape and that it had a bright future.

The provincial was perplexed by what had happened, the more so because in 1983 members of the province had enthusiastically attended a series of workshops on the charism of the congregation. He had heard participants saying things like: 'Our charism is highly relevant to the present age. . . . We have so much to offer people. . . . We have a grand future.' Yet, the province remained blind to the fact that it was dying.

In 1985 a new provincial took office and he immediately visited every member of the province over a three-month period. He reported to his advisers that the majority of the men were 'angry, often without quite knowing why . . . fatalistic about the future . . . blaming various people for the present malaise in the province . . . not at all anxious to look too closely at what must be done to face the future . . . denying the need to change'. The province, he reported, 'is drifting from crisis to crisis, grieving over losses already suffered and those that are fast approaching, but all the while feeling guilty about the grieving'. He saw that his major task over a three-year period would be to lead the province through rituals of mourning. The workshops on the founding charism appeared successful, he concluded, simply because they reinforced in participants a sense of false identity and relevance. The workshops did not challenge them, he felt, to face the nitty-gritty of taking the charism creatively into the world beyond the province, leaving the old and apostolically irrelevant to die in peace.

He and his advisers decided, after seeking skilled advice, to develop a co-ordinated province-wide ritual of mourning. They recognized that successful chapters depended on the depth of preparation over a long period; a process of individual and corporate conversion was desperately needed. Consequently, the following plan was devised and initiated:

—more executive staff were employed to take the administrative load off the provincial.
—the provincial team began regularly to pray together, sharing their pain over the losses being experienced personally and corporately, and praying for the gift of listening to the Lord.
—a pastoral planning team was selected that would involve each house/apostolate in a process of looking at pastoral needs and resources.
—superiors were invited to attend a workshop to learn the art of liturgical mourning rites so that they could lead their communities to face grieving constructively; the mourning rites were structured according to the pattern found in the lament psalms (see explanation in Chapter 4), with ample time being given over to the 'complaint' phase to allow participants the chance to express their feelings about the losses in the province/community.

—the provincial team invited several suitable and pastorally creative people to investigate the possibility of a new apostolate based on the urgency of pastoral needs and the availability of the province's resources.

After nine months of investigation and a further three months of training, three religious established a new apostolate well away geographically from other works of the province.[11] The distance and clear lines of accountability to the provincial allowed the men to apply themselves to the new challenge without unnecessary distraction; the provincial leadership team kept the province informed of each step in the new project's progress.

—at regular local or province-wide gatherings of congregational members liturgical mourning rituals were arranged; every effort was made to involve participants and people skilled in liturgical processes.

—at rituals of celebration, for example, at jubilees of religious, the provincial highlighted the creative, pastoral and community contributions of the people involved.

—the regular newsletters by the provincial to the province were used to explain various pastorally creative projects being undertaken by members.

Three years after the initiation of this co-ordinated rite of passage for the province, the leadership team evaluated what had been happening. On the positive side, the provincial chapter of 1989 was a far more faith-oriented gathering than any previous chapter, and the manpower realities of the province were confronted calmly and without denial. Overall, members of the province seemed more personally at peace, far less fatalistic than before about the future, and rather proud of the new pastoral project—for it showed them that something pastorally constructive and new could be done, even with limited resources. No longer did members say that *the* challenge of the province is the need to recruit new members; instead, people seemed more at ease with the stress on Gospel-quality life coming from the provincial team.

Negatively, the provincial and his team recognized that they sometimes moved too quickly to prevent people individually and corporately from experiencing the chaos of disintegration of old and irrelevant ways of doing things. They had not realized that the process of grieving takes considerable time and that the stages cannot be precisely plotted or anticipated. Secondly, they had placed far too much hope in the potential of superiors to lead their communities in prayer and rituals of mourning. Superiors needed to be better selected, trained, regularly called to be accountable for their leadership according to definite criteria, and encouraged to develop personal support systems. Thirdly, the provincial leadership team had failed to develop sufficiently an ongoing evaluation of their own work; too much time at team meetings was being given over to crisis issues and insufficient to forward planning and the ongoing evaluation of the province-wide ritual of mourning.

Fourthly, the team recognized that far more time had to be set aside for prayer and to periods of relaxation together, otherwise some decisions would continue to be made without due reflection. On the issue of prayer, they admitted that, by trusting too much in their own human skills of leadership, they were ignoring the warning of Moses given to the Israelites: 'Beware of thinking to yourself, "My own strength and the might of my own hand have given me the power to act like this". Remember Yahweh your God; he was the one who gave you the strength to act effectively like this. . . . Be sure: if you forget Yahweh your God, if you follow other gods . . . you will perish' (Dt 8:17–19).

Summary

The process of refounding Gospel communities has nothing directly to do with seeking an increase in membership. Certainly we want people to join us, but refounding is primarily a question of the revitalization of Gospel-quality living. Hopefully, if God wishes, people will be attracted to join us because of our sincere efforts to live out the Gospel life.

We need refounding and creative people to lead us in this process of refounding. We also need skilled administrators. A key function of administrative heads is to be ritual leaders of community mourning. The qualities of such leaders are well portrayed in the life of the prophet Moses. He had to use his persuasive gifts in relating to his own people (Ex 4:27ff.) and to Pharaoh (Ex 5) without being able to use force. Only his faith and gifts of administration could win success. Throughout the journey in the desert Moses illustrates how a skilled ritual leader can help people break away from the bondage of the past, formulate and communicate a vision of the future, and inspire people to journey through the intervening chaos.

Discussion questions

1. Does the group agree that we must 'refound Gospel communities' in today's Churches? If not, why not? Does *your* Gospel community need refounding?
2. Why is the willingness on the part of a Gospel community to undertake a ritual of grieving a crucial condition for refounding?
3. What is the relationship between prayer and creative grieving?
4. Does your group take sufficient time and space to pray?
    What are the factors that facilitate and/or obstruct the sharing of faith and prayer within *your* group?
5. In addition to Moses, are there other influential ritual leaders in the Old Testament? What lessons do they give us for our own group's life?

References

1. *The Prophetic Imagination* (Philadelphia: Fortress Press, 1978), pp. 110, 113.
2. John Paul II, 'Peace with God the Creator: Peace with All of Creation', *The Tablet* (UK) (6 January 1990), p. 29.
3. *Out of Chaos; Refounding Religious Congregations* (New York: Paulist Press, 1988), pp. 88–111 and *passim*. Integral to the thesis I present is the role of the individual in change. H. G. Barnett summarizes an applied anthropology conclusion: 'All cultural changes are initiated by individuals. The stimulus for a new idea or a new behavior is consequently always specific to a given individual . . .': *Innovation: The Basis of Cultural Change* (New York: McGraw-Hill, 1953), p. 39.
4. Brueggemann, *The Prophetic Imagination*, op. cit., p. 110.
5. See ibid., p. 113.
6. See Arbuckle, *Out of Chaos*, op. cit., pp. 112–35.
7. See G. A. Arbuckle, *Earthing the Gospel: An Inculturation Handbook for Pastoral Workers* (London: Geoffrey Chapman, 1990), pp. 81–95.
8. See C. M. Martini, *Through Moses to Jesus: The Way of the Paschal Mystery* (Notre Dame, IN: Ave Maria Press, 1988), *passim*; N. M. Sarna, *Exploring Exodus: The Heritage of Biblical Israel* (New York: Schocken Books, 1987), pp. 38–220.
9. *The Prophetic Imagination*, op. cit., p. 111.
10. Administrators may be helped to appreciate the need for outsider special-

ists by the following authors: J. F. Benson, *Working More Creatively with Groups* (London: Tavistock, 1987); R. Scott Sullender, *Grief and Growth: Pastoral Resources for Emotional and Spiritual Growth* (New York: Paulist Press, 1985), pp. 116–67.

11. I call this approach 'the pastorally new belongs elsewhere'; see Arbuckle, *Out of Chaos*, op. cit., pp. 40, 125.

EPILOGUE

... do not grieve ... as others do who have no hope
(1 Th 4:13).

I urge you, then, brothers and sisters, ... Do not model your
behaviour on the contemporary world, but let the renewing of
your minds transform you, so that you may discern for yourselves what is the will of God—what is good and acceptable and
mature (Rom 12:1f.).

There is a painting by Jan Vermeer, a seventeenth-century
Dutch artist, of the scene at Emmaus in which Jesus is breaking
bread with the two disciples. Like much of Vermeer's work,
there is in this painting a subtle manipulation of light so that
it blurs the outlines of objects and the figures; there is also a
deliberate use of perspective to embrace the viewer in the
scene. Through these brilliant techniques he captures the heart
of the Emmaus incident because the viewer senses in the painting an atmosphere of both sadness and joy. And at the same
time the observer feels that he or she has frequently lived this
same experience: the discovery of Jesus in moments of sadness
and joy in the viewer's journey of life.

The Emmaus story, as depicted by the evangelist Luke, is a
magnificent ritual of individual and community grieving, with
a pattern in its movement akin in some important aspects to
that found in any lament psalm. This is why Vermeer's painting is so moving and relevant for all times. He is able to
convey the sadness and joy of a perfect ritual of grieving in
which Jesus is ritual leader, as he was in his own suffering
and death. Readers, accept the invitation of Vermeer and allow
yourselves in this epilogue to be drawn again into the Emmaus
happening. The main insights of this book will be summarized
as the pattern of the incident is explained.

The evangelist Luke is recording the social drama[1] of the
Emmaus event, because the Christian communities he writes
for in the ninth decade of the first century are finding it difficult to recognize the presence of the risen Lord in the midst
of their persecutions and problems.[2] They need an inspiring
example of how to grieve over their own blindness and failures

to acknowledge the mighty power of the Lord to save them. God in Christ can do the impossible! They must let go of their narrow worldly ways of looking at life to allow the hope and joy of the risen Lord to enter into their lives.

The Emmaus story opens with the first stage of a ritual, the separation period. The two disciples representing the views of the community of early believers are disappointed, angry, and discouraged because of everything that had happened to their leader. In theory they knew that Jesus had 'resolutely turned his face towards Jerusalem' (Lk 9:51); in this, the breach stage of the social drama of our redemption, he had uncompromisingly set himself on a collision course with all who would reject his teaching. The two disciples would also have heard of the crisis point of the social drama, when Jesus had spoken with sharp clarity to the apostles after the Last Supper about his coming death. He would not turn away from the painful mission given him by the Father:

> I shall not talk to you much longer, because the prince of this world is on his way . . . (Jn 14: 30).

> You will be weeping and wailing while the world will rejoice; you will be sorrowful, but your sorrow will turn to joy. . . . Now I am leaving the world to go to the Father . . . (Jn 16:20, 28).

The two disciples and other members of their faith community would have remembered these words, but in their grief they still failed to comprehend their meaning.

So, Jesus, as the skillful ritual leader, gently approaches the two grieving disciples as they walk away from Jerusalem, and he deliberately encourages them to articulate their feelings of disappointment and anger over the shattering of their dreams of a worldly kingdom: 'What are all these things that you are discussing as you walk along?' (Lk 24:17). Several verses are given over to their cries of lament (vv. 17–24); they blurt out the whole miserable story of their unrealized dreams: 'Our own hope had been that he would be the one to set Israel free . . . [but] our leaders handed him over to be sentenced to death, and had him crucified' (vv. 21, 20). Jesus then draws them into the liminal period of the ritual, in which he both berates and confronts them with their own denial and misreading of the events: 'You foolish men! . . . Was it not necessary that the Christ should suffer before entering into his glory?' (vv. 25f.). They have been seeing the Good News as bad news, with their hearts attached to a worldly vision of the role of Jesus. They must discard this false set of expectations of Jesus.

The final point of the liminal experience is the breaking of bread, in which Jesus the guest appropriates to himself the role of the host and leads the group in prayer and the breaking of the bread. The disciples are finally converted. In the depths of their hearts they become one with Jesus as he relives his own passion 'and their eyes were opened and they recognised him; but he had vanished from their sight' (v. 31). They die to a very human way of looking at Christ's death and are seized in return by a hope and a joy that seemed totally impossible a few hours before.

Now comes the moment of reaggregation to the wider community. The disciples, with the enthusiasm of the newly converted after a very dramatic liminal experience, rush to tell the little Christian community, who they had earlier left in deep confusion and sorrow over Christ's death, what has just happened to them:

> ' Did not our hearts burn within us as he talked to us on the road and explained the scriptures to us?' They set out that instant and returned to Jerusalem. . . . Then they told their story of what had happened on the road and how they had recognized him at the breaking of bread (vv. 32–35).

Strengthened by participation in this ritual of grieving, the two disciples and others begin the process of refounding their community of faith. The lesson to us is: 'Jesus said . . . "Go, and do the same yourself" ' (Lk 10:37).

References

1. For an explanation of social drama, see Chapter 2 above.
2. See J. A. Fitzmyer, *The Gospel According to Luke (X–XXIV)* (New York: Doubleday, 1985), pp. 1554–69; and E. LaVerdiere, *Luke* (Dublin: Veritas Publications, 1980), pp. 284–288.